T4-AQK-831

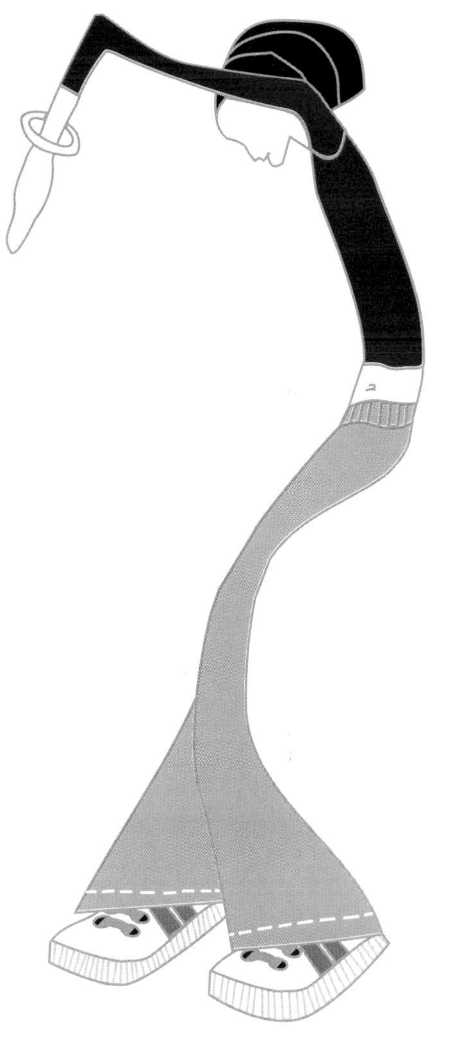

Samantha's Oracle

A Fortune Teller for Teenage Witches

Samantha Hardie

This book is dedicated to my best friends in the world – Emma, Holly and Pippa;
and to my incredible mother, Titania Hardie, without whom I could not have done this xxxxx.

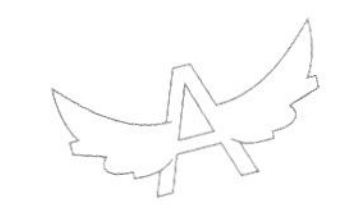

contents

Introducing Samantha, the Teenage Witch

Hi, nice to see that you picked my book for your bookshelf. I'm Samantha (Sam to my friends), and this is just to tell you a little bit about the book and myself.

I have grown up in a very magical and mystical environment with oracles and fortune cards all around me. You may know my mom, Titania Hardie. She has become a very well-known witch. She wrote the adult oraqle (spelled with a "q" not a "c" because this is a lucky magic letter). But I felt it was time that we changed it for us teenagers to answer all those questions that no one else can.

My own oraqle is not hard to use. As long as you pick a question true to your heart, it will give you the right answer.

Remember, take your time: it is the magic inside you that will find the right answer, not the magic of turning the page.

I hope you enjoy my oraqle.

Samantha Hardie

On the opposite page you will see a box of nine symbols. On the next two pages there are 66 questions.

First, pick your question from the list on pages 8 and 9, **then turn back to the box of symbols.** Close your eyes and hold the hand you write with a little bit above the symbols.

Move your hand in a circular motion over the box, **and think hard about your question until you feel your hand drawn down to a symbol.** Now open your eyes to see which symbol you have landed on.

Make sure that you remember your question number and the symbol you have landed on, **then turn to page 10 to discover how to find your answer.**

CHOOSE A QUESTION FROM THIS LIST

1. Is the problem at school going to go away?
2. Will I ever have a boyfriend?
3. Will I do well on the test at school?
4. Can I trust ..... with my secret?
5. What does the next year hold in store?
6. Are my pimples ever going to go away?
7. Will I get the money I need for .....?
8. Do my friends really like me?
9. Will my interview go well?
10. Am I ever going to find clothes I look good in?
11. Why hasnt my friend called me?
12. Does ..... still like me?
13. Should I go to .....'s party?
14. Will my friend ever give my ..... back?
15. How can I make it up to ..... for what I've done?
16. Do I look fat?
17. Is the work I'm finding so hard going to get easier?
18. Will ..... call me soon?
19. Will my vacation be romantic?
20. Will I ever be happy with my body?
21. Have I made the right decision?
22. Is something in my life going to change soon?
23. Does ..... really dislike me?
24. Can ..... help me with my problem?
25. Will I have children?
26. Will I have a successful career?
27. What is just ahead for me?
28. Is everything going to go OK at .....?
29. When is my period going to start?
30. When will my parents realize that I am no longer a child?
31. Will ..... trust me again?
32. What should my good luck charm be?
33. Are my parents going to stop quarreling soon?
34. Is ..... really serious?
35. Can I be sure that my plan will work?
36. Is ..... cheating on me?
37. Do my friends really believe that?
38. Should I say I'm sorry first?

39. What do people really think of me?
40. Is my package coming soon?
41. Is this going to last forever?
42. Should I really believe .....?
43. Is my future love interest good-looking?
44. Is everything going to be OK?
45. Will I be famous?
46. Am I going to have fun?
47. Is this ..... going to settle down?
48. What is my parents' problem?
49. Is good luck coming my way?
50. Will my friends be happy for me?
51. Are ..... and ..... ever going to like each other?
52. Is ..... going to cause me problems?
53. Will my friend forgive me?
54. How do I get out of this mess?
55. How do I make ..... stop upsetting me?
56. Does ..... even notice me?
57. What does my relationship future hold?
58. Why is ..... so cold with me?
59. Is this rumor true?
60. Will I ever be rich?
61. Is someone gossiping about me?
62. Can I find what I am looking for?
63. Is everyone picking on me at the moment or is it just me?
64. Does ..... like me for who I am?
65. How do I get closer to .....?
66. Will my present happiness last?

Now turn to page 6 to ask the Oraqle your question

HOW AND WHERE
TO FIND YOUR ANSWER

Opposite and on the next two pages you will see a chart that you can use to find the page on which your answer is written. Along the top of the chart are the symbols and down the side are the numbers of the questions. Find your question number down the side (for questions 23-66 please turn the page), then find the symbol you landed on along the top. Run your finger down the column that has your symbol at the top of it and run another finger across the line with your question number in it. Where they cross you will find a box with the page number of your answer. Turn to that page and you will see the box of symbols. Find the symbol you landed on and there you will find your answer.

Run your finger down the column of the symbol you landed on. Then run a finger of the other hand across the row beginning with your question number. Where they cross is the page number for your answer

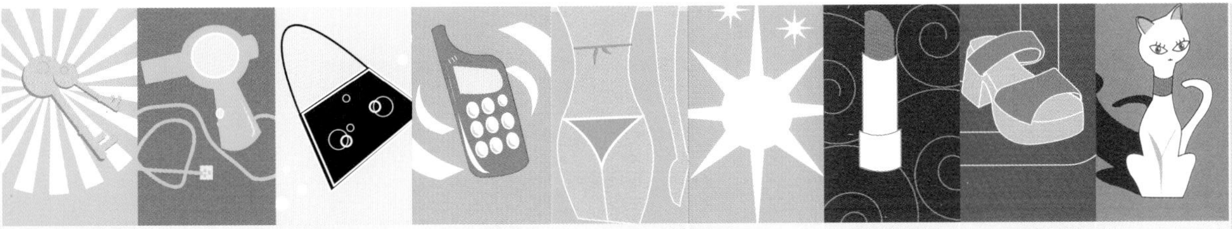

Question Numbers									
1	19	25	31	37	43	49	55	61	67
2	20	26	32	38	44	50	56	62	68
3	21	27	33	39	45	51	57	63	69
4	22	28	34	40	46	52	58	64	70
5	23	29	35	41	47	53	59	65	71
6	24	30	36	42	48	54	60	66	72
7	25	31	37	43	49	55	61	67	73
8	26	32	38	44	50	56	62	68	74
9	27	33	39	45	51	57	63	69	75
10	28	34	40	46	52	58	64	70	76
11	29	35	41	47	53	59	65	71	77
12	30	36	42	48	54	60	66	72	78
13	31	37	43	49	55	61	67	73	79
14	32	38	44	50	56	62	68	74	14
15	33	39	45	51	57	63	69	75	15
16	34	40	46	52	58	64	70	76	16
17	35	41	47	53	59	65	71	77	17
18	36	42	48	54	60	66	72	78	18
19	37	43	49	55	61	67	73	79	19
20	38	44	50	56	62	68	74	14	20
21	39	45	51	57	63	69	75	15	21
22	40	46	52	58	64	70	76	16	22

Run your finger down the column of the symbol you landed on, then with the other hand run across from your question number. Where they cross is the page number for your answer

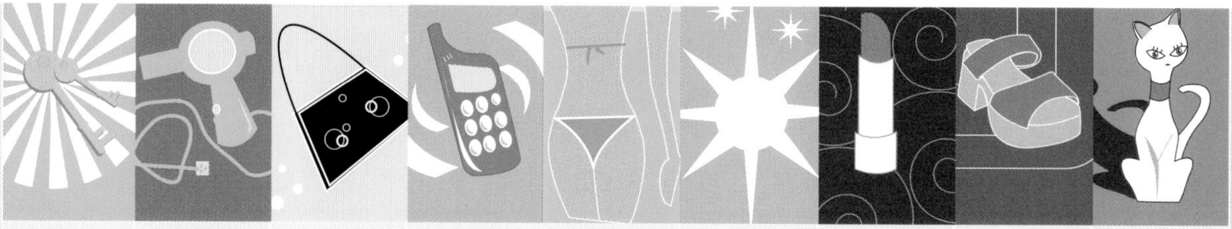

Question Numbers									
23	41	47	53	59	65	71	77	17	23
24	42	48	54	60	66	72	78	18	24
25	43	49	55	61	67	73	79	19	25
26	44	50	56	62	68	74	14	20	26
27	45	51	57	63	69	75	15	21	27
28	46	52	58	64	70	76	16	22	28
29	47	53	59	65	71	77	17	23	29
30	48	54	60	66	72	78	18	24	30
31	49	55	61	67	73	79	19	25	31
32	50	56	62	68	74	14	20	26	32
33	51	57	63	69	75	15	21	27	33
34	52	58	64	70	76	16	22	28	34
35	53	59	65	71	77	17	23	29	35
36	54	60	66	72	78	18	24	30	36
37	55	61	67	73	79	19	25	31	37
38	56	62	68	74	14	20	26	32	38
39	57	63	69	75	15	21	27	33	39
40	58	64	70	76	16	22	28	34	40
41	59	65	71	77	17	23	29	35	41
42	60	66	72	78	18	24	30	36	42
43	61	67	73	79	19	25	31	37	43
44	62	68	74	14	20	26	32	38	44

Run your finger down the column of the symbol you landed on, then with the other hand run across from your question number. Where they cross is the page number for your answer

Question Numbers									
45	63	69	75	15	21	27	33	39	45
46	64	70	76	16	22	28	34	40	46
47	65	71	77	17	23	29	35	41	47
48	66	72	78	18	24	30	36	42	48
49	67	73	79	19	25	31	37	43	49
50	68	74	14	20	26	32	38	44	50
51	69	75	15	21	27	33	39	45	51
52	70	76	16	22	28	34	40	46	52
53	71	77	17	23	29	35	41	47	53
54	72	78	18	24	30	36	42	48	54
55	73	79	19	25	31	37	43	49	55
56	74	14	20	26	32	38	44	50	56
57	75	15	21	27	33	39	45	51	57
58	76	16	22	28	34	40	46	52	58
59	77	17	23	29	35	41	47	53	59
60	78	18	24	30	36	42	48	54	60
61	79	19	25	31	37	43	49	55	61
62	14	20	26	32	38	44	50	56	62
63	15	21	27	33	39	45	51	57	63
64	16	22	28	34	40	46	52	58	64
65	17	23	29	35	41	47	53	59	65
66	18	24	30	36	42	48	54	60	66

It may be
gone forever.

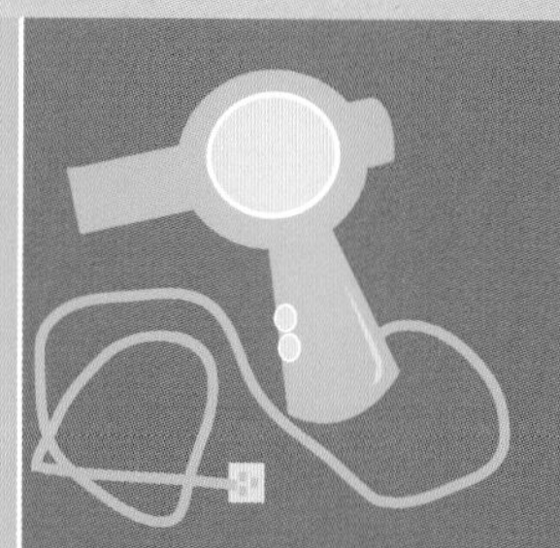

Not really.

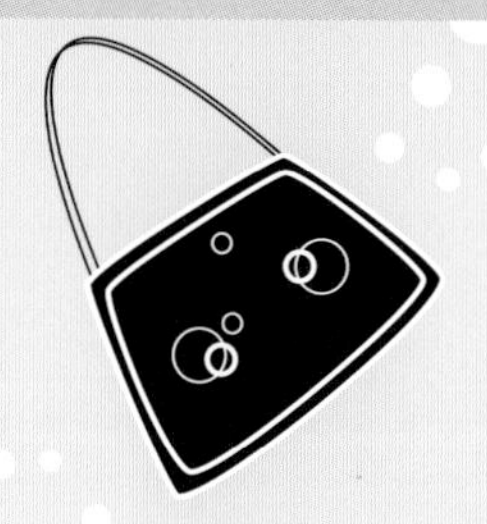

More jealous
than happy.

This has hurt very
deeply, actually.

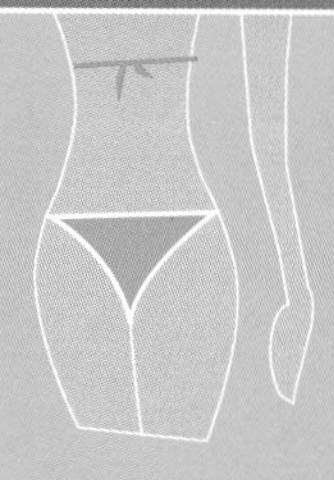

If you don't, you risk
losing a friend.

Ask someone close to
you in your family.

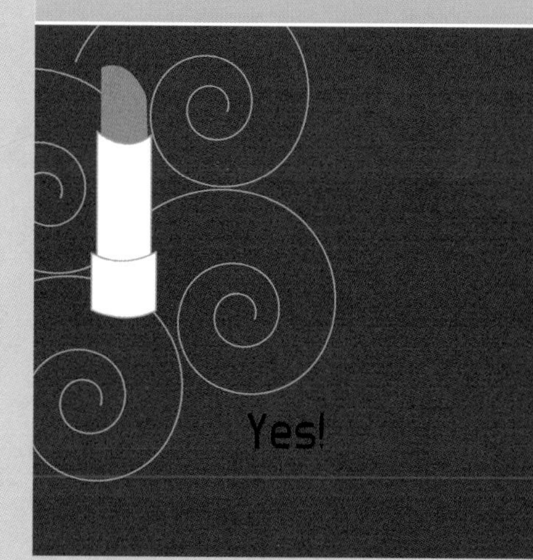

Yes!

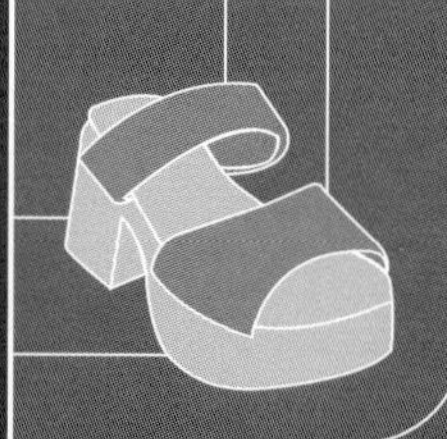

All you need is a little
more confidence.

You've loaned your
friends things before.
You know what happens.

It is just you worrying.

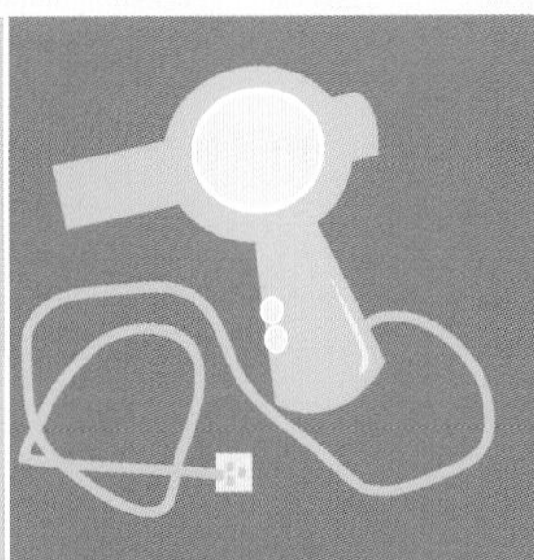

A few romances
and one serious love.

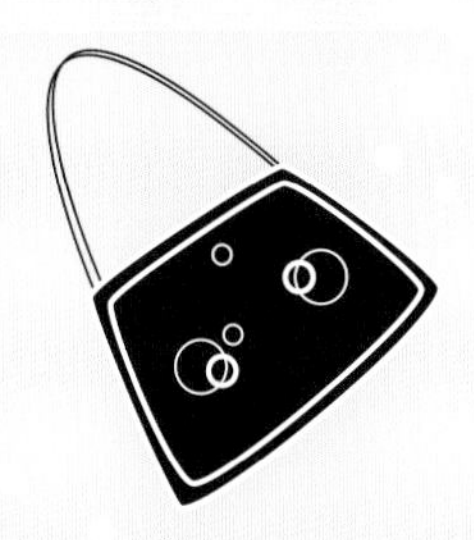

Not very likely.

Not you but someone
in your family.

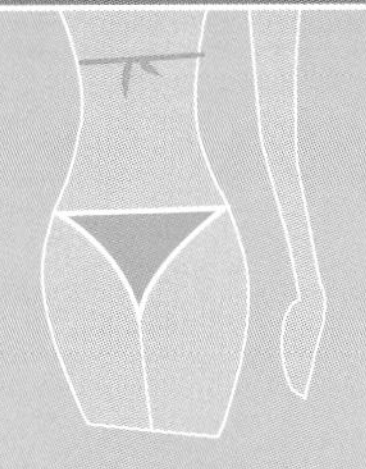

That you are
completely crazy!

They need to get it all
out; you have to live
with this a little longer.

A wish come true.

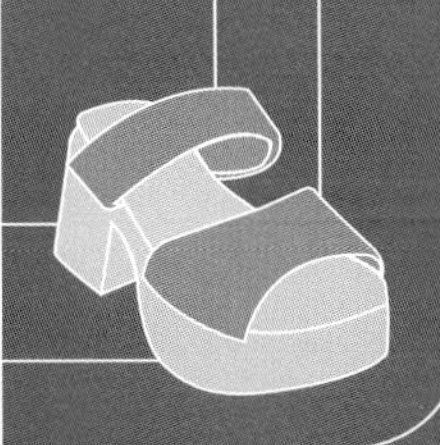

This decision
will help a lot of
people around you.

It is not serious, but
they have to make it up
to you too. Talk about it.

Very much.
Conflict of opinion.
No.
Not always.
It seems to be lost.
Don't worry:
it is not the truth.
It is a temporary
disaster, but you'll
laugh later.
No change, which
is not necessarily
a bad thing.
No. You are
naturally large,
tall, and strong.

This is as close
as you get.

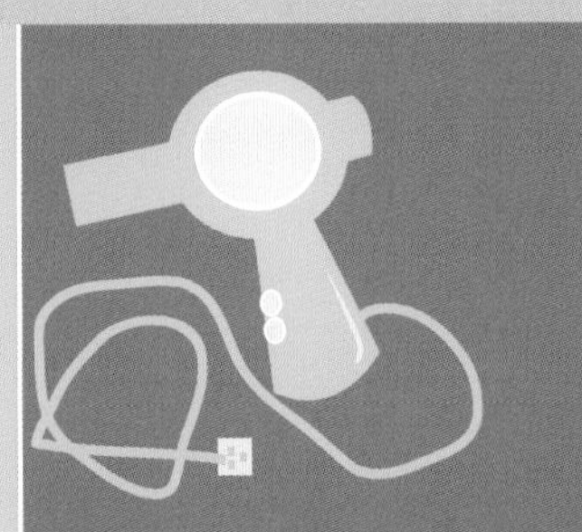

Sort of.

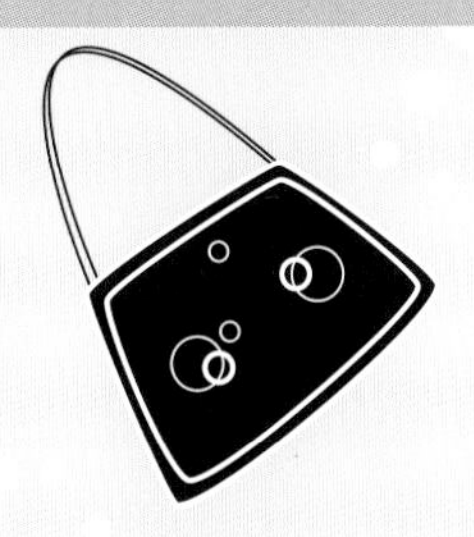

They already have.

It will definitely
settle down soon.

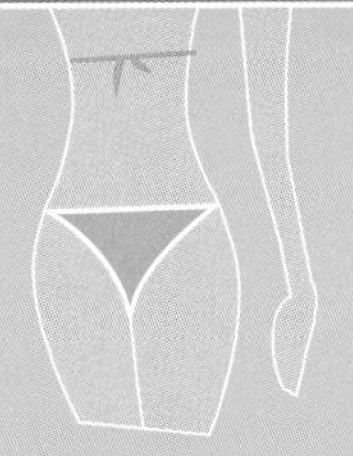

I'm afraid not.

You may have to
wait to find out.

Any day, any moment.

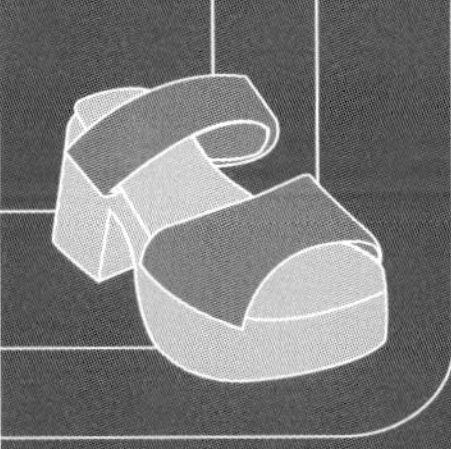

Yes.

Ask someone
close for a little help.

For a long time.

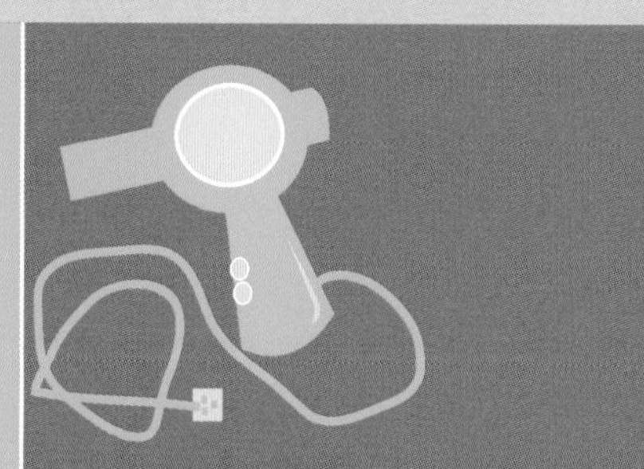

Not really.

With a little help from your friends.

They don't want you to grow up too fast.

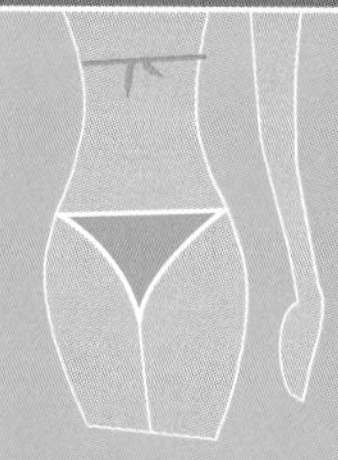

You really know it's true.

Not yet, but someone close *is* trying to hurt you.

By your next birthday.

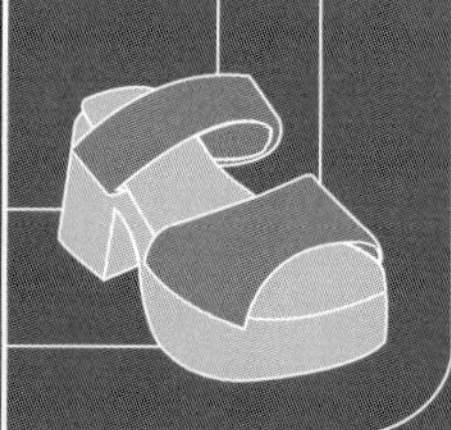

Yes, definitely.

Not soon, but they will call.

In time, yes.
A little.
Ignore them.
They will get bored.
Unusually for you, yes.
Not really, but it won't
matter at all!
Not your closest friends.
Definitely.
You'll look after many,
but they won't
all be yours.
It depends on
whether you let
your guard down.

You already have one.
If you look hard enough.
They are shyer than you are.
Very happy.
It all depends on you.
You're the braver one if you do.
The one you had when you were little.
The work you do will be more satisfying than successful.
You don't even need to ask that question!

Only if you study hard and are sure you know the subject.

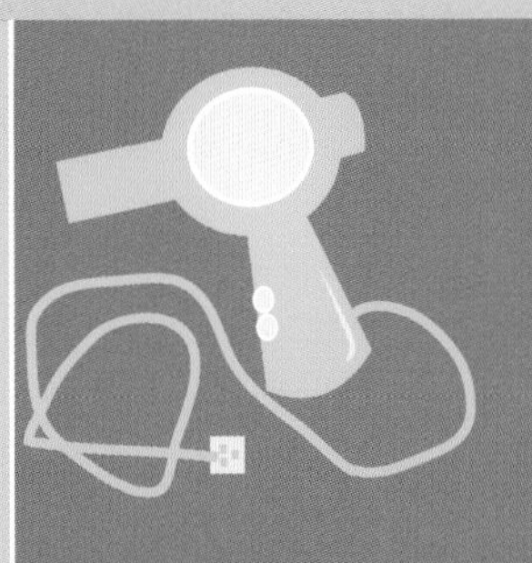

A little of both.

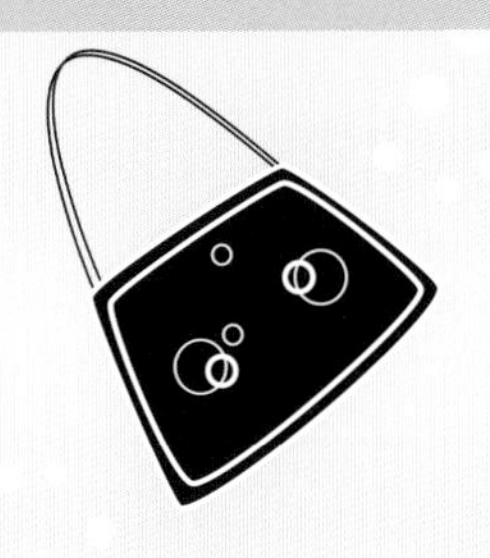

A lot of romances!

It's up to you.

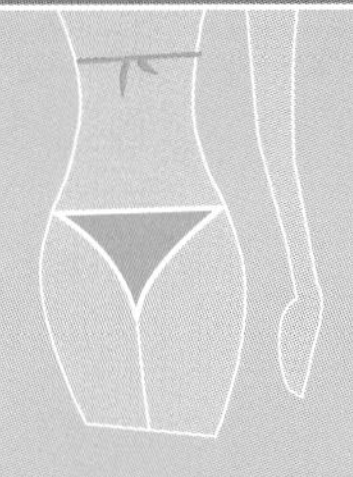

You may be, a little.

Most people like the way you make them laugh.

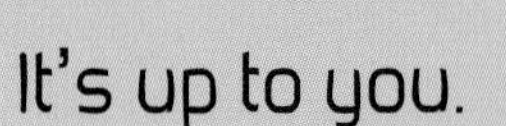

They will stop; but afterward, things may not end as you wish.

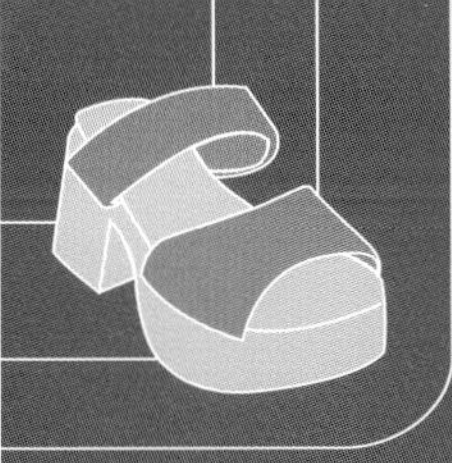

A friend is in pain. Help.

Your decision may come back to haunt you a little.

Not with this one.

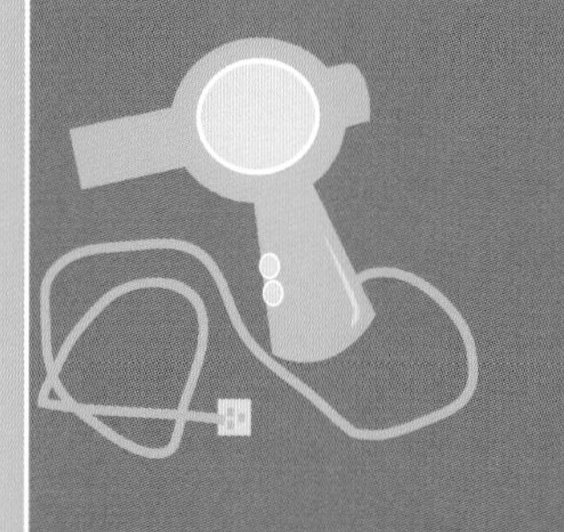

Yes.

You are so similar.

I'm afraid so.

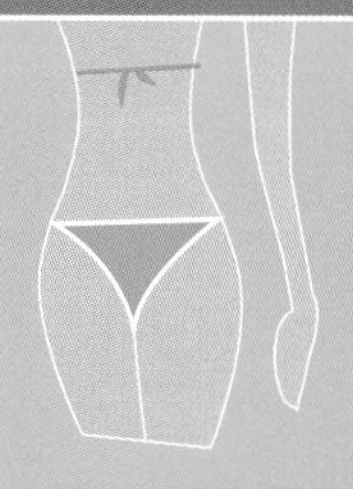

You are the life
of the party.

This package may
never turn up.

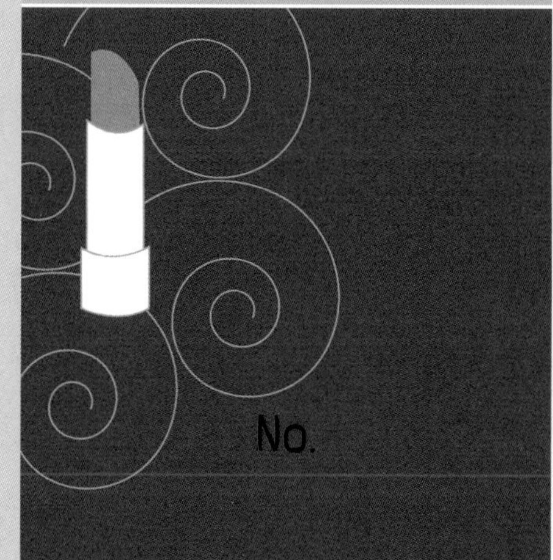

No.

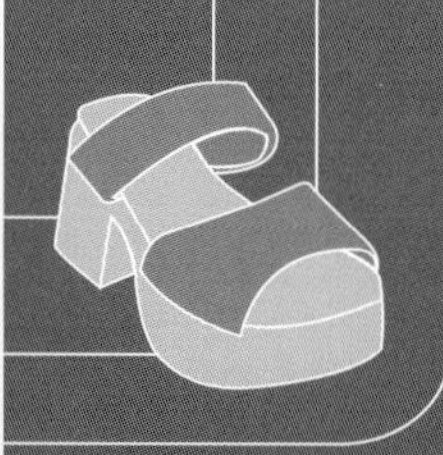

It could go either way.

Not for you, but for
someone close.

A romance.
By showing them who you really are.
Not really.
You have really hurt them.
It still has to work itself out.
No, just a little while longer.
If you have all the details right.
Very soon; be patient.
Don't worry about this now.

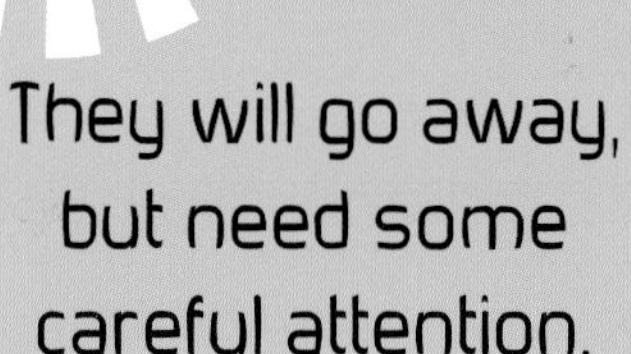

They will go away, but need some careful attention.

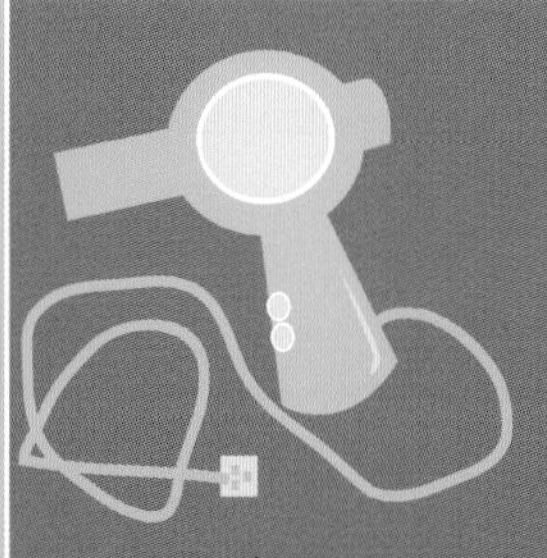

Not much longer, but something else exciting will replace it.

Not very rich, but comfortable.

It will work itself out in the end.

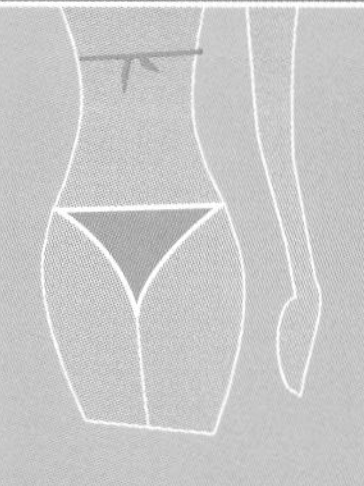

It is your problem, not theirs.

It is not the full story.

Don't believe what other people say.

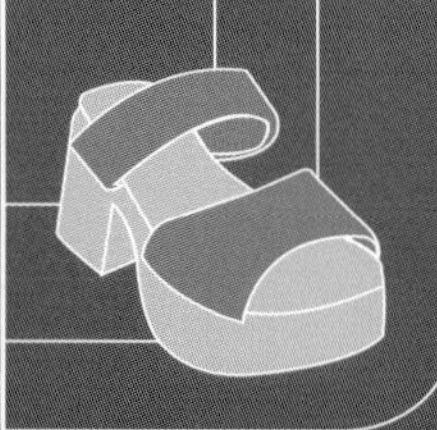

They are trying, but you can help.

Ask a few people, not just one. You will get a better result.

It may take hard work, but yes, you will.
It's up to you.
Not at all.
Tell someone.
A year of good luck.
Too handsome. Everyone will want a piece!
Yes.
Yes.
Possibly not.

Yes, very much.
In time.
It does not wish
to be found.
Do you really
want them to?
Not totally.
Things will change.
No. Wait for an apology,
but accept it warmly.
A heart.
Don't you already have
one developing?

Yes, you are well prepared. Good luck.
It will be difficult, but you will.
No, it's everyone else.
True love.
They don't have to.
You may not be famous, but your name will become well known.
You're a bundle of fun.
No, they will continue for a while.
Some news.

You already have good taste. Relax!
Be careful how much you tell.
Not really.
They just don't like you.
Not likely.
If you relax.
It has only just been mailed.
Yes.
Yes.

Your friend has
not been at home.
Give them a chance.

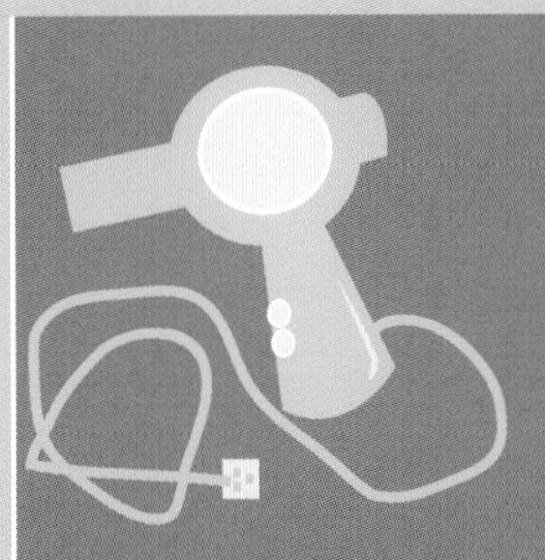

An exciting journey.

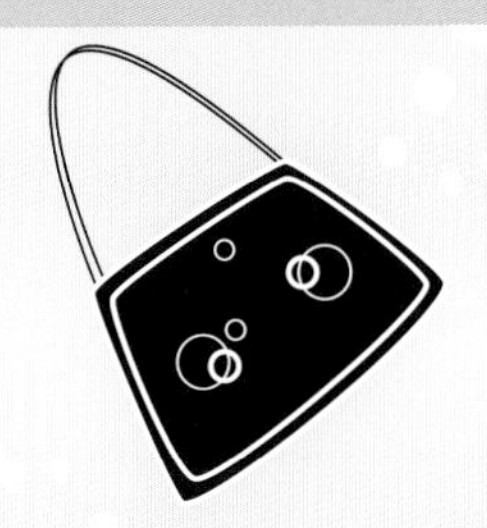

Stop trying to be
someone else.

Positively.

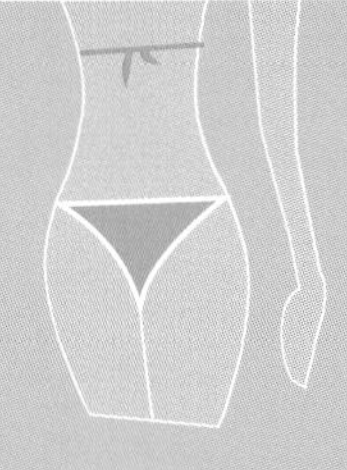

If you say you're
sorry fast!

Say something
to help heal it.

Yes.

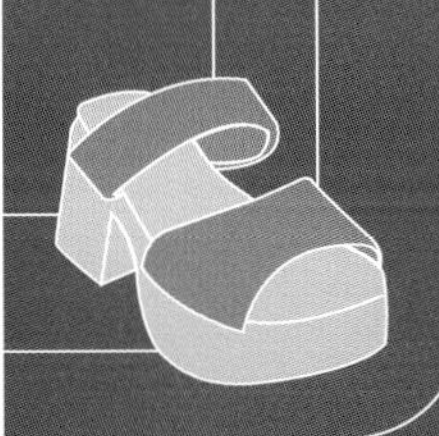

You will have to
work hard for the
result you want.

You already know the
answer to that.

Yes, they have just had no spare time recently.
You have hardly any, so don't worry.
Yes. For as long as you want it to.
You will never be in need of anything.
The same way you got into it.
One they will have to work out on their own.
They are just trying to make trouble.
They are not at all reliable.
Don't push. It's coming.

What is stopping you?
Probably not.
Not if you don't tell someone.
Yes. A lot.
Just walk away.
Your luck is never that bad.
You will have so many, it is hard to tell.
They'd like to!
Soon.

You took the risk of the loan; ask for it back.
Yes, even though it doesn't always seem that way.
Of course.
Maybe not.
Definitely!
In a way.
You need to approach the problem differently.
Meet them halfway.
Look beside your bed.

It's already forgotten.

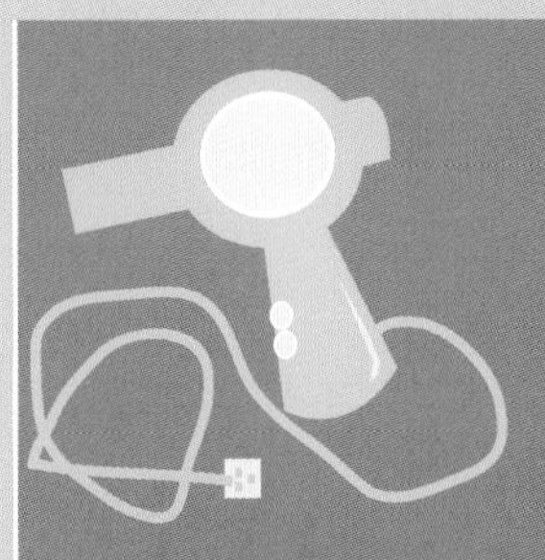

You will do fine.

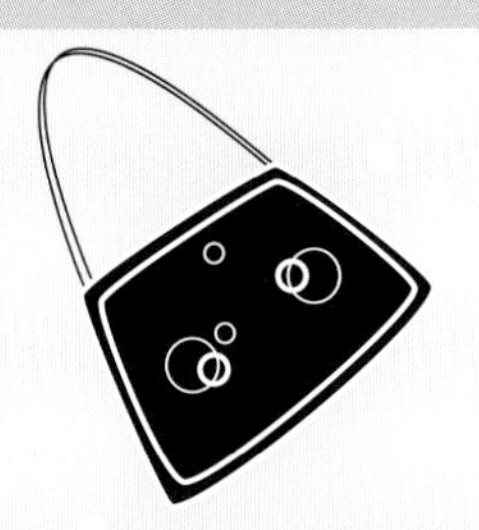

As long as you don't kid yourself about what you know.

You are being a little difficult at the moment.

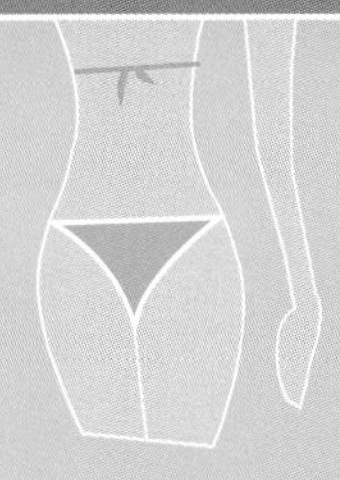

A disappointment.

They will, in time.

You'll be famous for being a terrific friend.

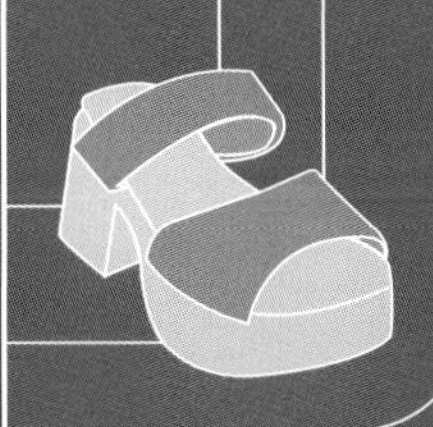

They think you're a great person, but that you can be moody.

Yes.

Don't worry.
You look fine.

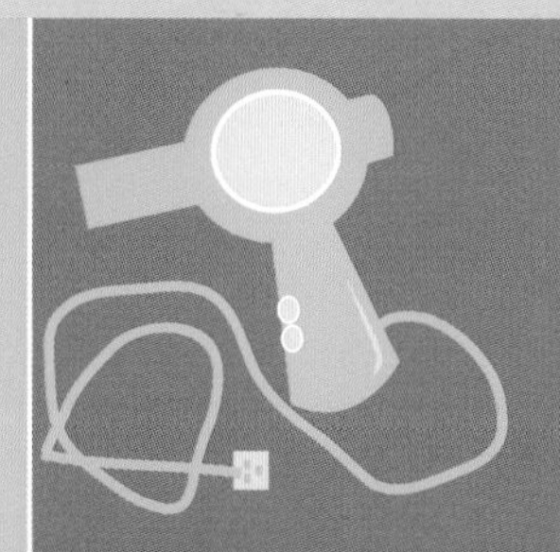

Shop and you shall find.

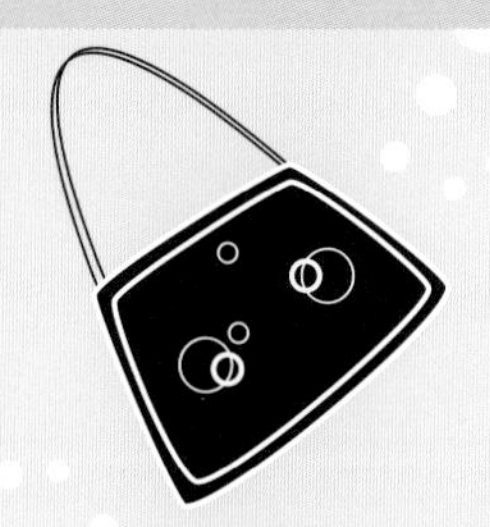

Why is this time different than last time?

Likes your popularity.

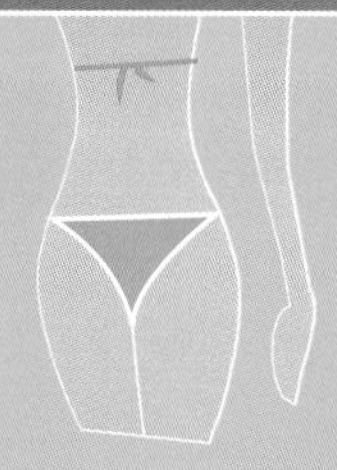

They don't want you to take their space.

They will do everything possible to make it hard for you, but you'll win.

If you want to.

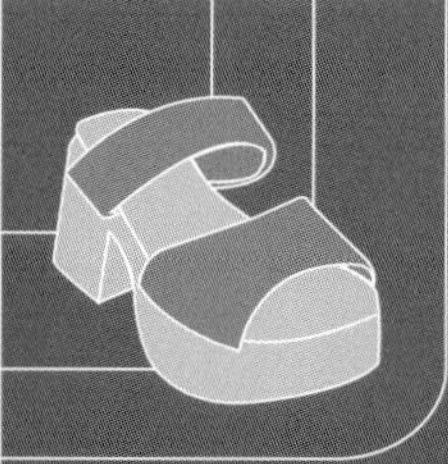

It will come when you stop looking.

Think about it.
You should know!

It will take time,
but it will get easier.

They explained
themselves.

Money seems to
be on the horizon.

You can't get close
to this person.

No.

Of course,
if you're honest.

You may have to
give it some time.

You know the answer
deep in your heart.

You will have to plan
your approach
very carefully.

It is on their list
of things to do.
They do like you, but a
little less than before.
They are natural.
Wait – they'll be gone
before you know it.
No. What makes you
happy will change.
You will have
enough money.
You are not
really in a mess.
Nothing for you
to worry about.
No, not at all.
Come out and ask them .

Not this one.

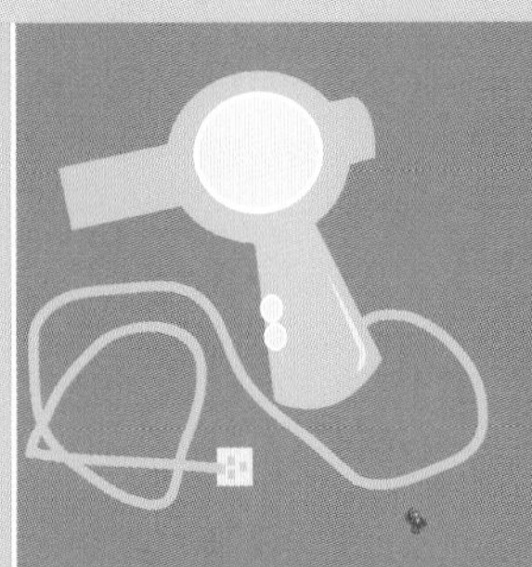

Yes, but nothing will happen.

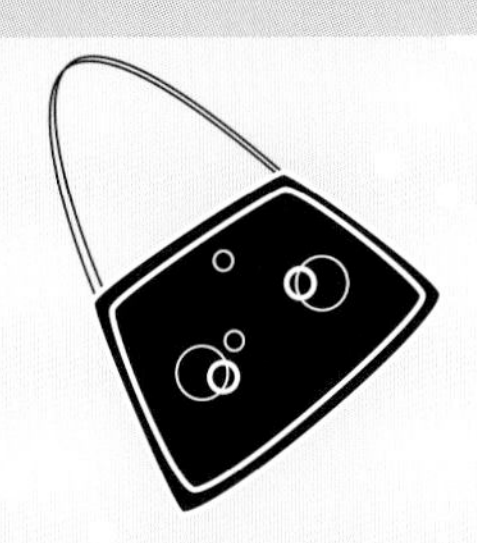

Someone will give it to you.

Yes.

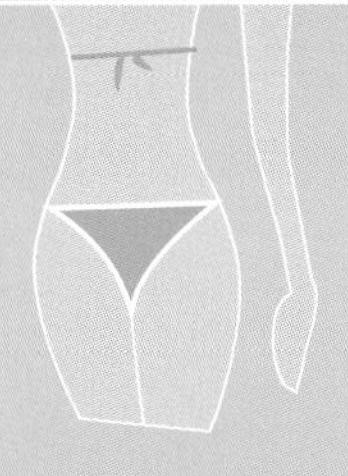

Yes, and you know who!

Think of a way of reversing the roles.

A little.

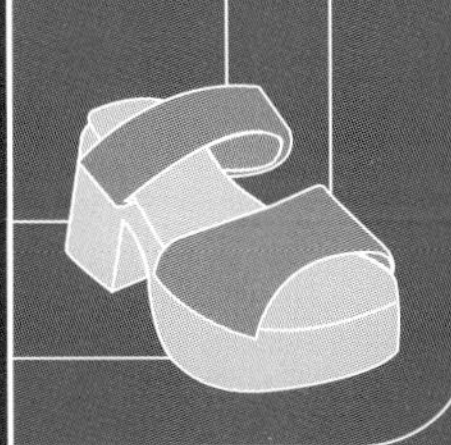

Yes; everyone will say so.

No, of course not.

You should be. You have a great body.

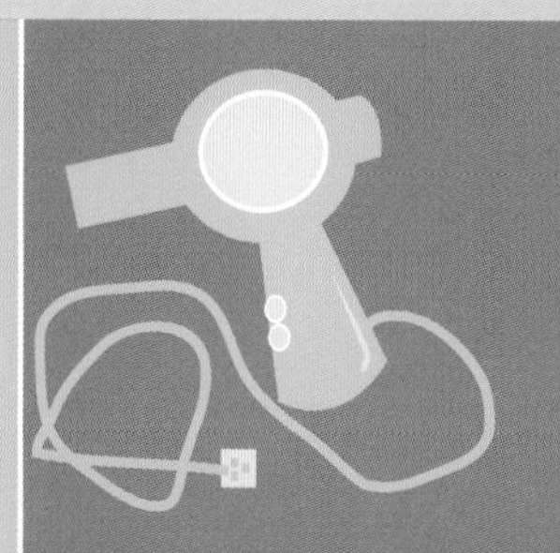

Unfortunately not.

Yes, but it's time for some new friends too.

Don't just want what someone else has. Your time will come.

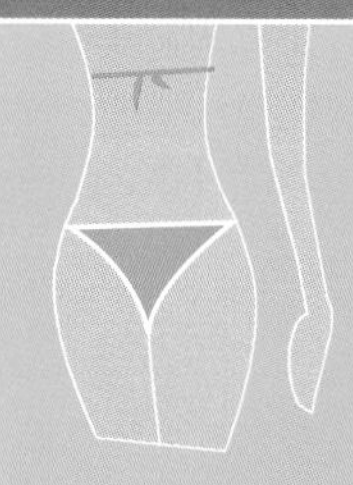

Sure you can; look again.

If you stop hiding, they will!

Some will.

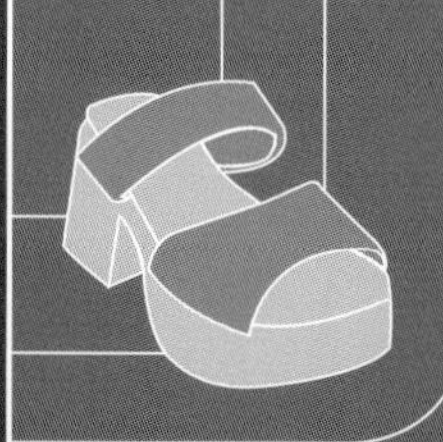

Not this time, but you'll soon stop regretting that.

Yes, quickly.

Yes, absolutely.

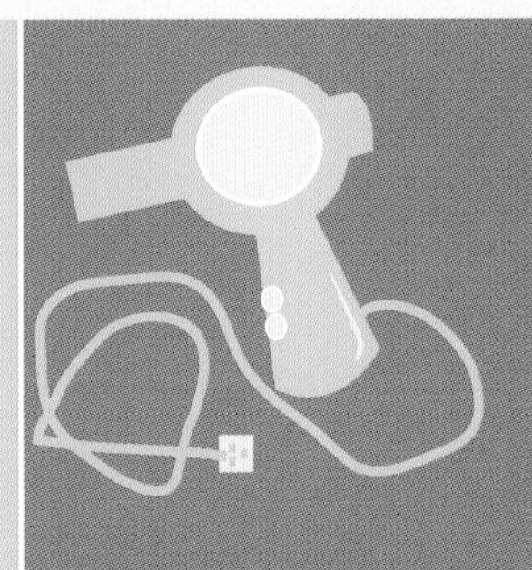

Only time will tell. But try.

Stop worrying. Everything is going to be fine.

You will be the one who decides that.

People are going out of their way to be difficult.

Much passion in love.

We shall see.

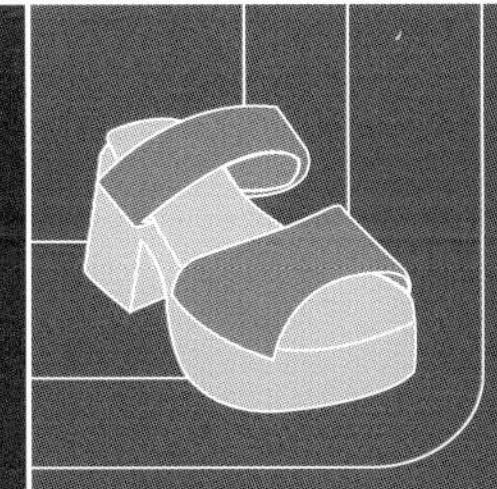

Yes: follow your dream.

Some think you're just too "purrfect," but those who know you, love you.

Something is going to change very soon.
You may have a little "puppy fat," but this will go if you eat healthy food.
Have more confidence. There are clothes out there for everyone.
Always.
Yes, but also for what you can do for them.
They see you as a threat.
No. They'll stay out of your way.
Yes. Lots of it!
Yes.

No, but you have very little in common.

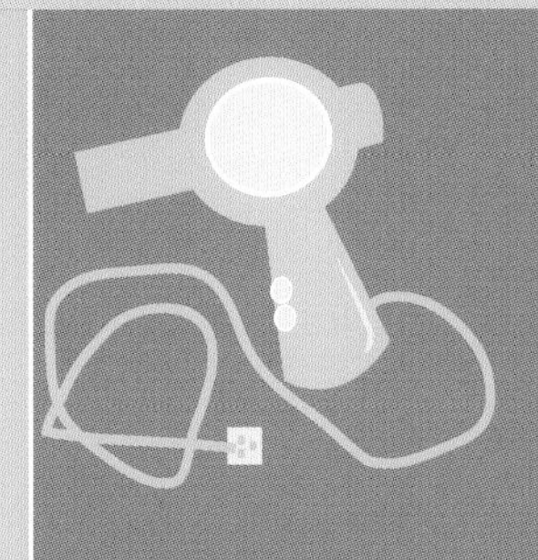

It will get worse, but then better.

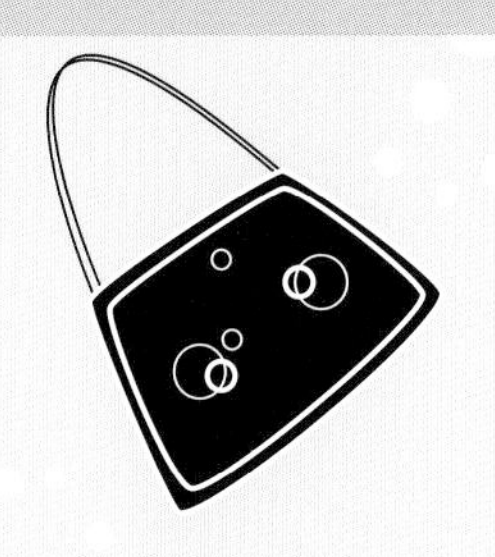

Your friend has been busy.

A new friend.

Just start as friends.

Very.

Wait a while and things will be fine.

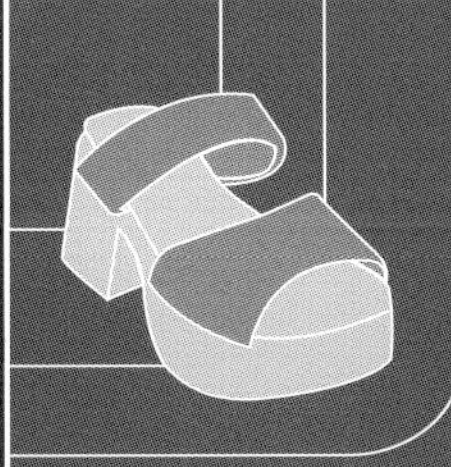

You need some good advice.

How long is forever?

A little; you have
to do the rest.

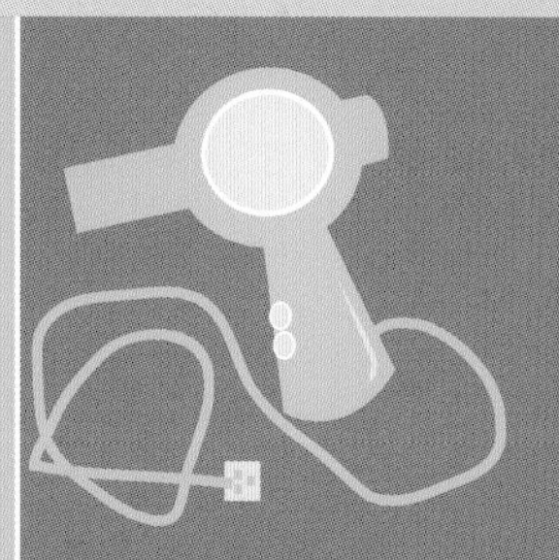

No. It has
slipped their mind.

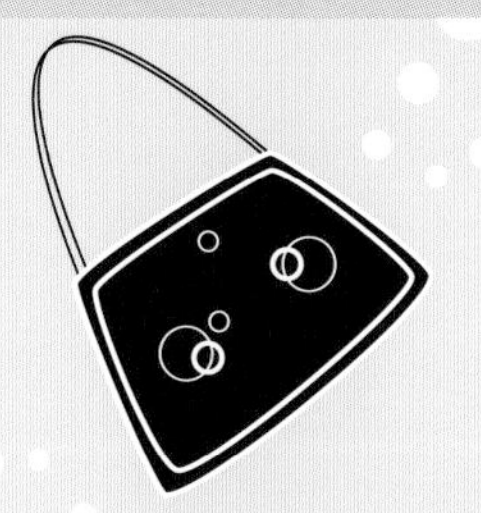

I believe that
question has been
answered for you.

They are already
responding to treatment.

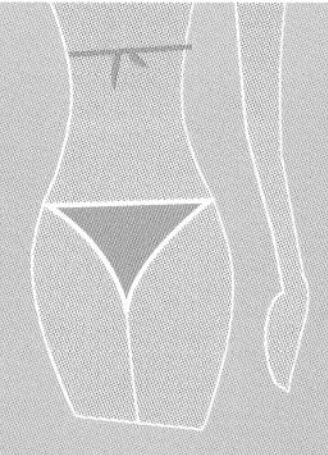

You will become
less excited about it.

It depends on what
you mean by "rich."

It is not
serious, so relax.

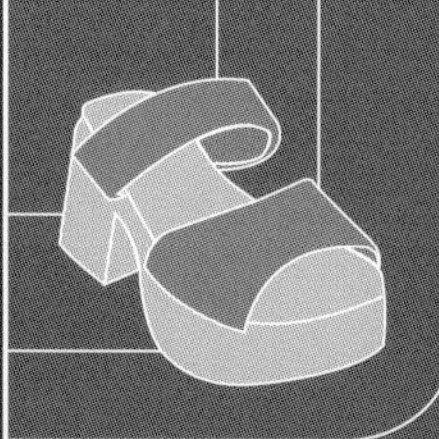

You know
exactly what it is.

For the moment, yes.

Yes.
Yes, very.
Don't worry about what others say. Go for it.
You will get it, but maybe not in time.
If you are brave and face it head-on.
Someone you should not worry about.
Someone at home will give you good advice.
Yes, something nice!
You know the answer to that.

A very successful one.
Not yet in your eyes, but believe what the people who care about you say.
Don't worry, it will find its way back to you.
Do you really need an oracle to answer that?
He will cause you problems, but yes.
No. It is gone forever.
No, but someone even nicer does.
If you include them in your happiness.
Yes.

An adventure.

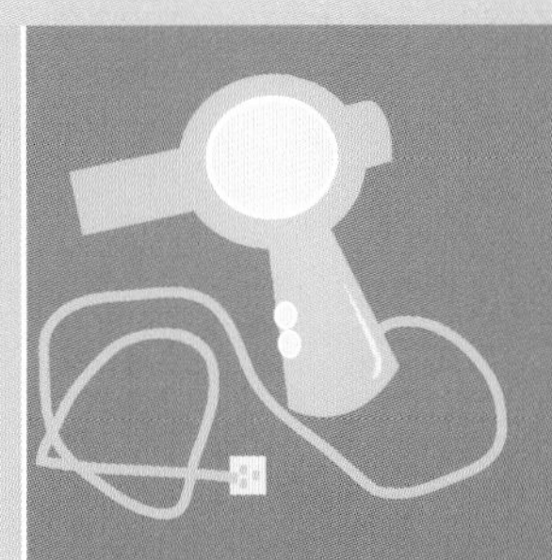

It may not be the wisest decision you ever made.

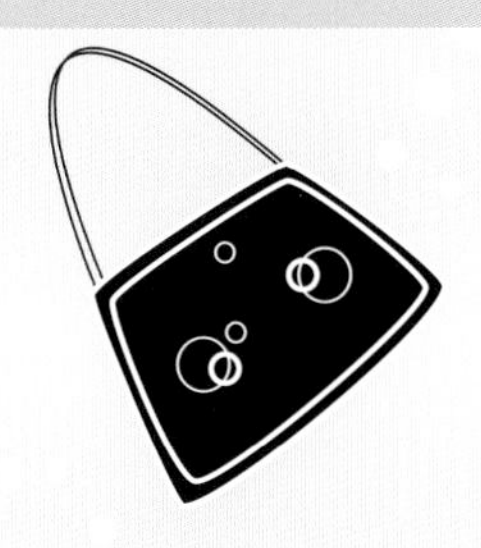

Give them space.

It will go well, but the result may not make you entirely happy.

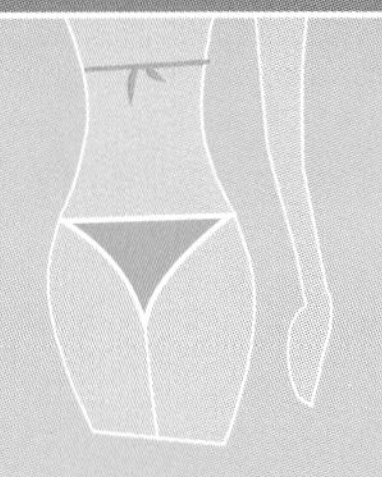

Not if you don't start studying now.

You are not very happy, so it just seems like it.

Someone to adore you.

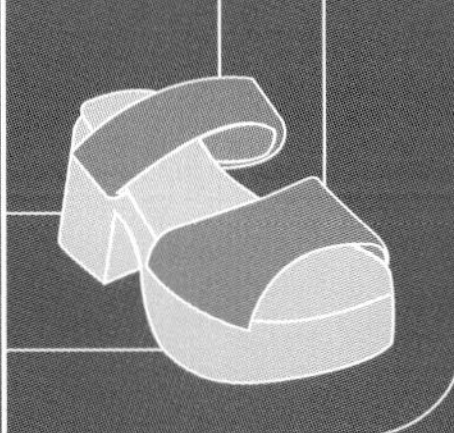

Yes, well enough.

If that's really what you want.

Everything will be wonderful.

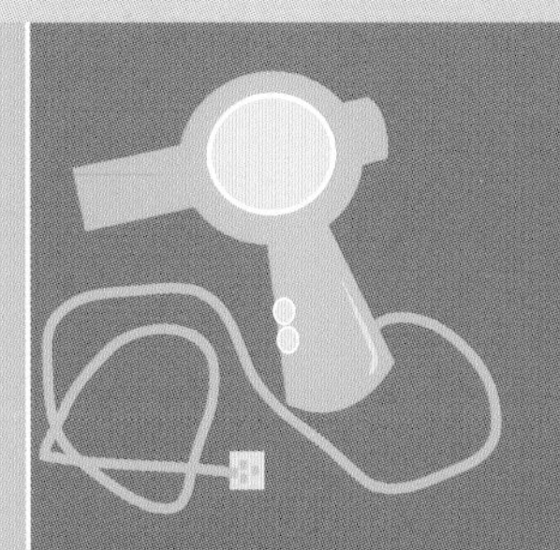

There are no changes in store at the moment.

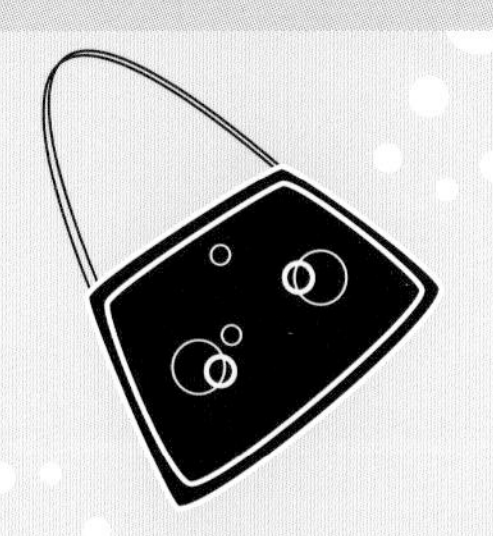

No. You're the right size and shape.

Of course. Everyone has a problem establishing their own style.

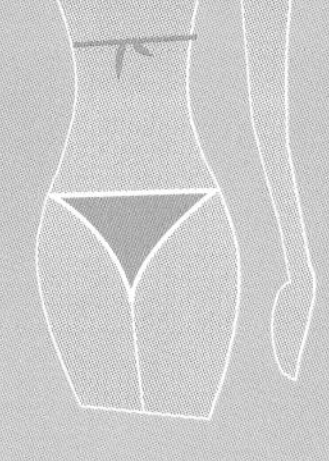

Think wisely about the secret you tell.

If you are asking this question, you are obviously unsure.

They don't understand you.

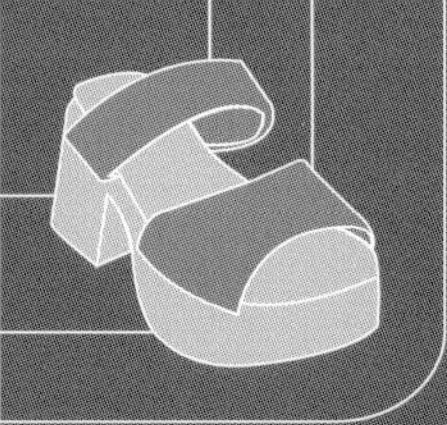

Possibly.

If you let yourself!

Soon.

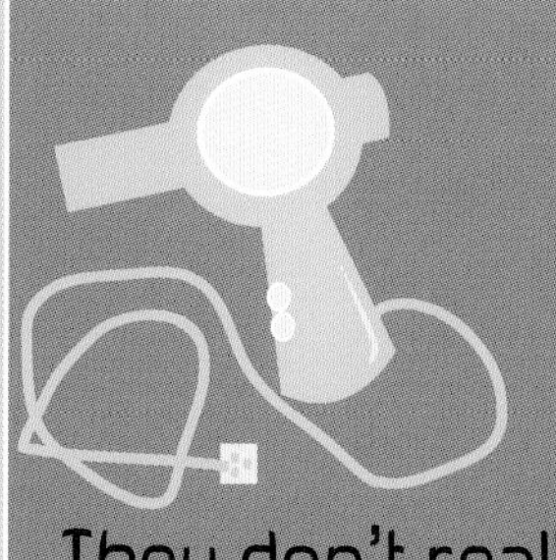

They don't really know you. Once they do, you'll get along better.

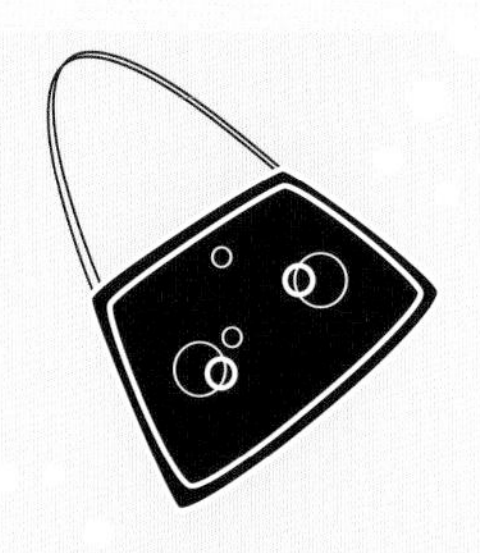

Yes, you are finding it hard because it's new to you. Give it time.

Because they have a problem at home.

An old wound will reopen when someone turns up from the past.

Someone else already has!

There is some truth in it.

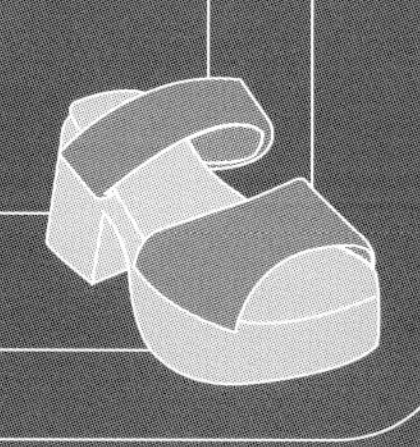

Once your friend has forgotten, there will be no problems.

Yes, and soon.

When you stop acting like one.
Of course, just ask.
It is difficult for them now, but they will call.
Not as much as you'd like, but someone close to them likes you a lot.
You know you need to watch what you eat, which will help a lot.
Yes!
Very, very rich.
There is a woman close to you. Ask for her help.
Your new friend.

Yes, in time.

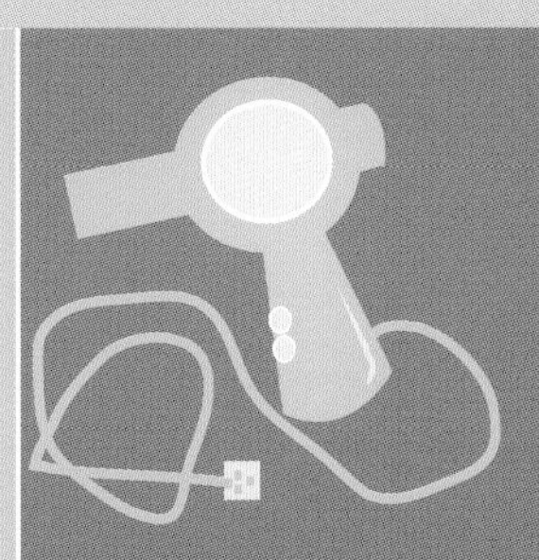

After a while you will.

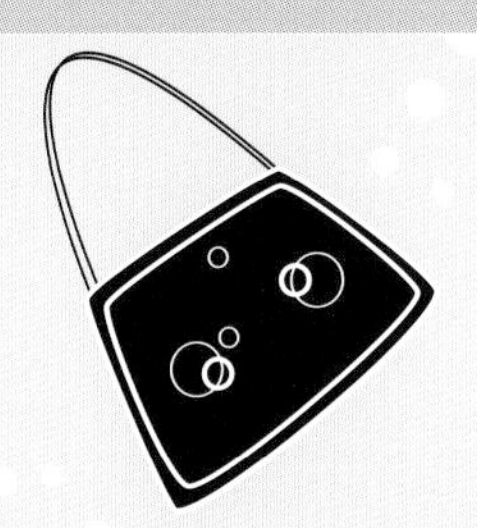

You will be
more interested
in other things.

This is a party
you could miss.

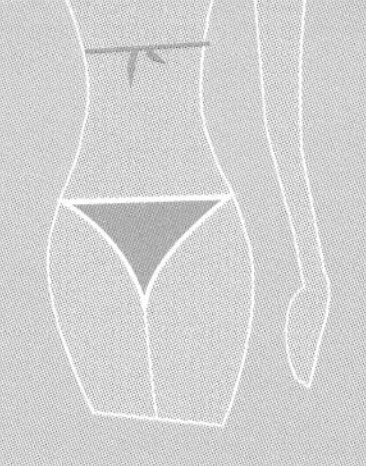

You have been working
hard to get it. Yes.

Your friends will soon
make you laugh about it.

They're only making
trouble. Ignore them.

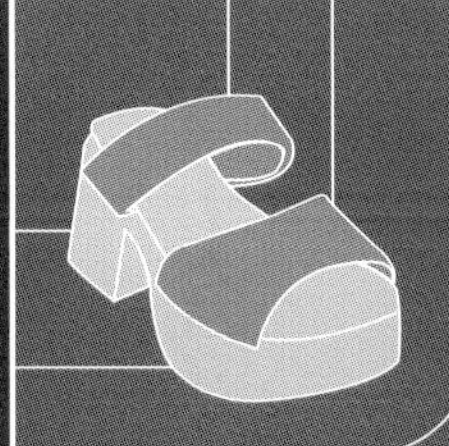

Be open, and
ask them to stop.

See your luck in smaller
things and you'll have
some tomorrow.

Try and find the one you have lost.

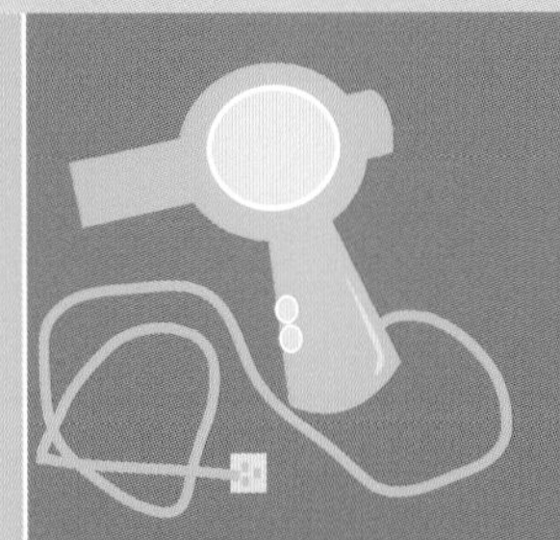

Successful yes, but not in the field you have in mind now.

Yes. You will get your body into great shape.

Your friend has become attached to it; you'd better replace it.

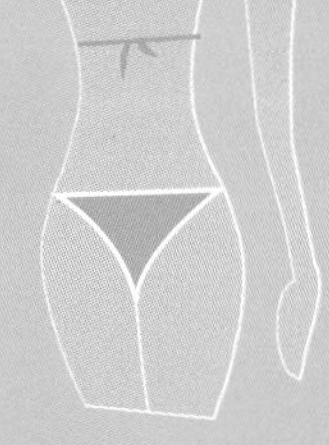

You have been joined at the hip for so long, they must!

Yes.

Look at home.

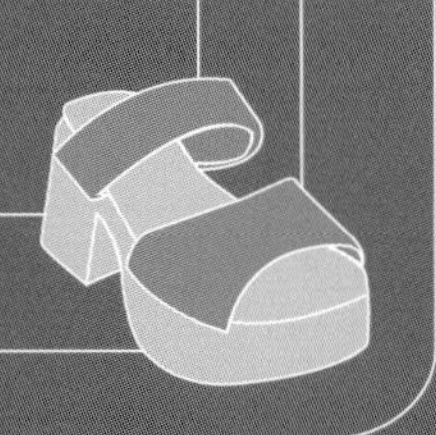

Yes, and you know it.

Absolutely delighted!

Let them work it out, and don't get involved.

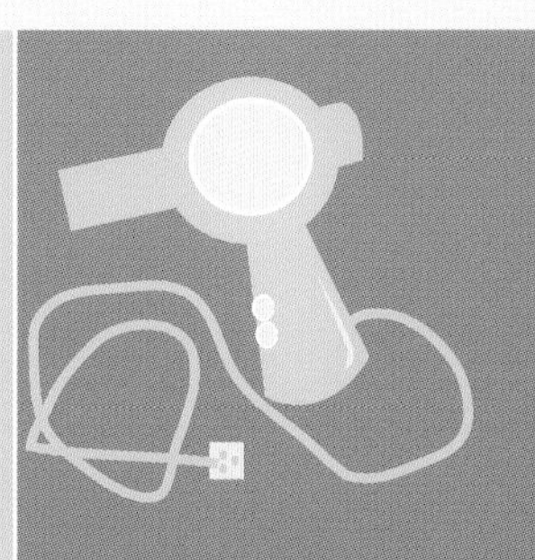

An important realization.

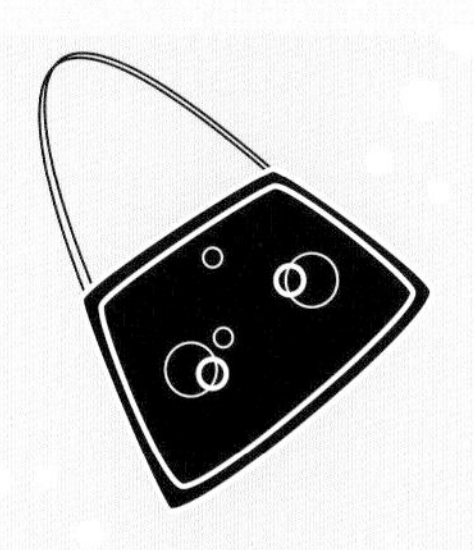

It was for the best.

They need to be sure that you're really sorry.

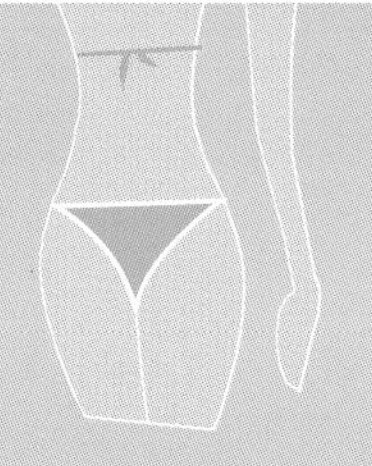

Not this one, but the next.

Yes, if you turn up on time and feel rested.

No, it is not you.

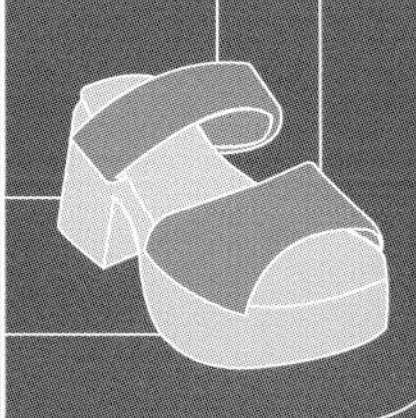

A lot of fun, but nothing too serious for a while.

Not really.

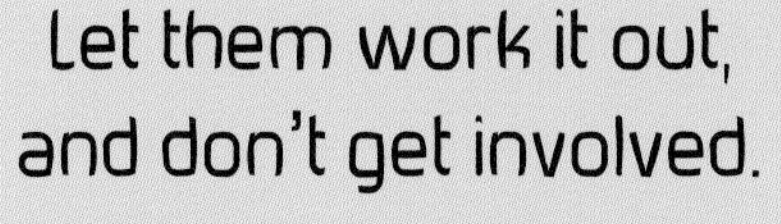

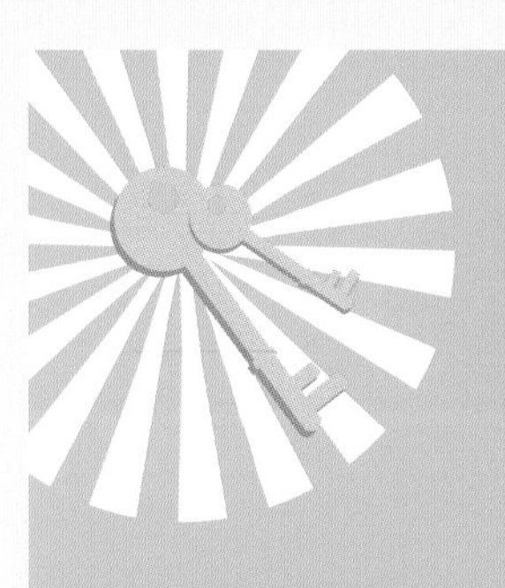

It may be a joke, but
probably not.

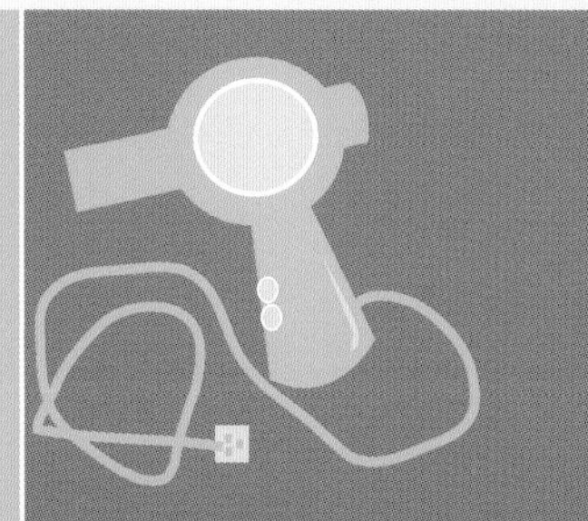

There will be
a minor hiccup.

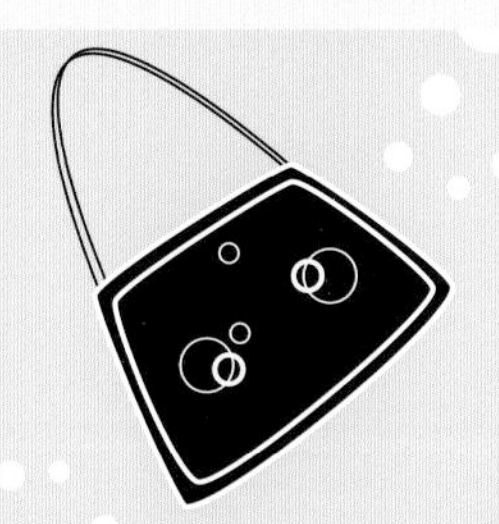

Yes, but it may not make
you completely happy.

Some clothes make you
look heavier, so choose
things that flatter you.

Try looking in a
new place, and
take a friend along.

Of course.
You always will
be able to.

Yes, but they've got a
funny way of showing it.

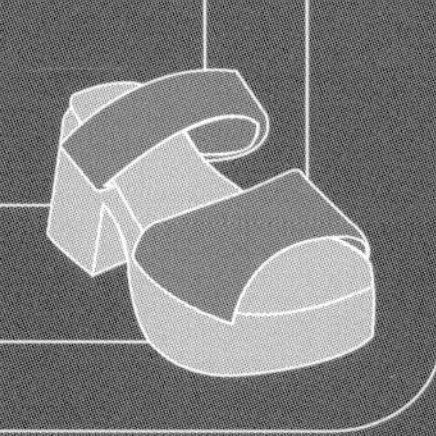

Because they
like you so much.

Actually, they will
end up helping you.

99%.

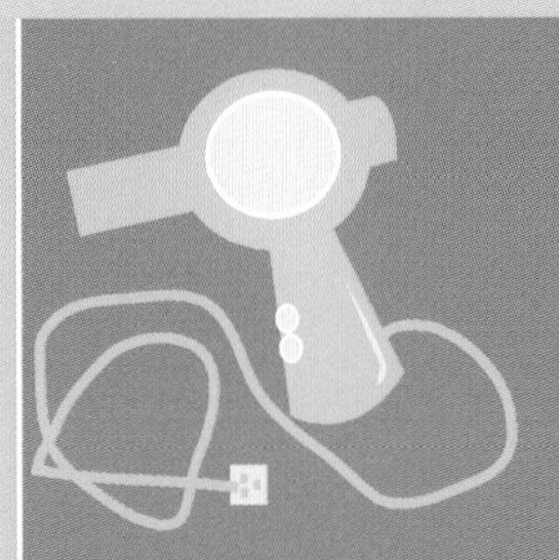

You may have
to wait a while.

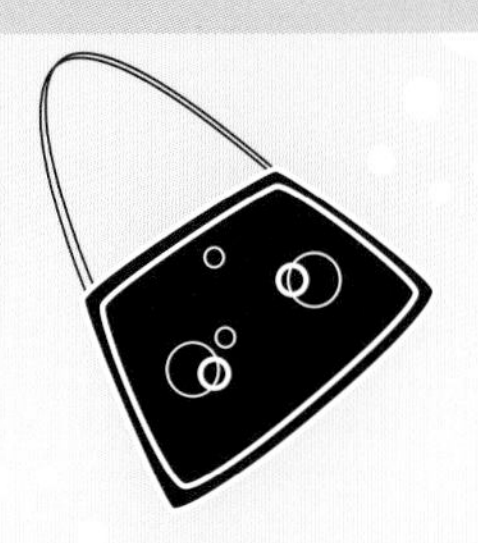

You are so similar
that you clash.

Unfortunately it may
continue to be hard for a
while, but keep trying.

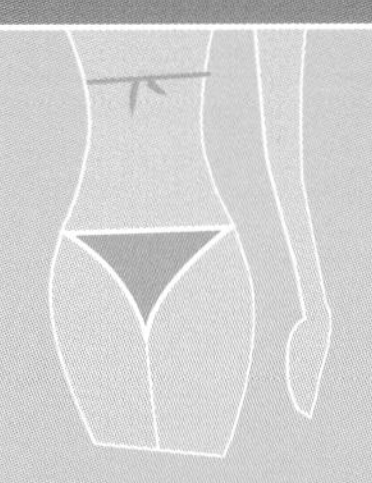

Your friend is wondering
the same thing!

An excellent
academic year.

You probably won't.

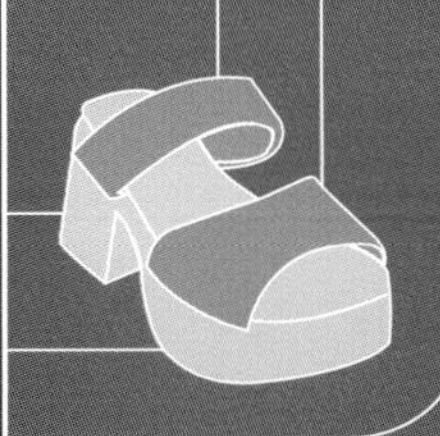

Yes, and you must
decide what to do.

Yes. This is a
passing problem.

It does seem so.

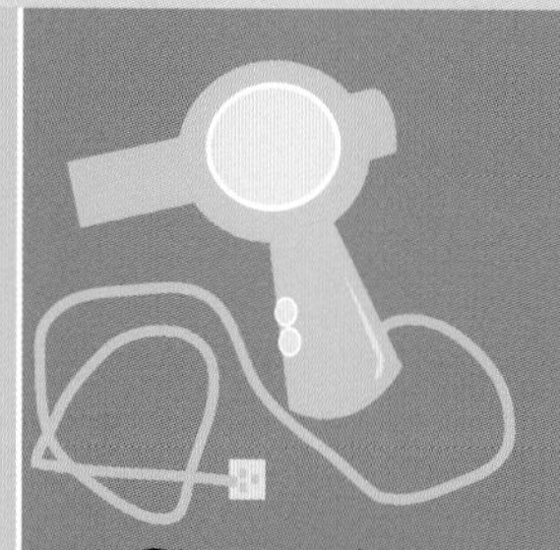

They already have. You just have to realize it yourself.

Maybe. But you may find someone else who deals with it better.

Something has come up that will postpone the call.

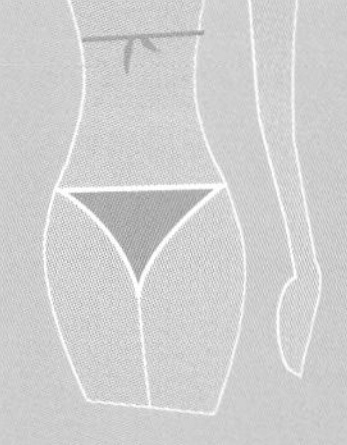

Absolutely, and you will know it soon.

It will take a little time.

Try to make it last; it depends on your attitude.

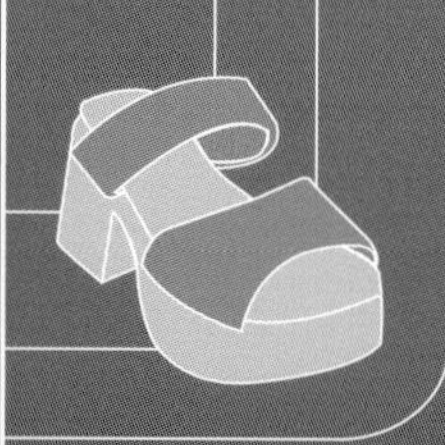

Yes. You'll always be lucky with money.

The answer is very close to home.

Only those who are not your true friends.

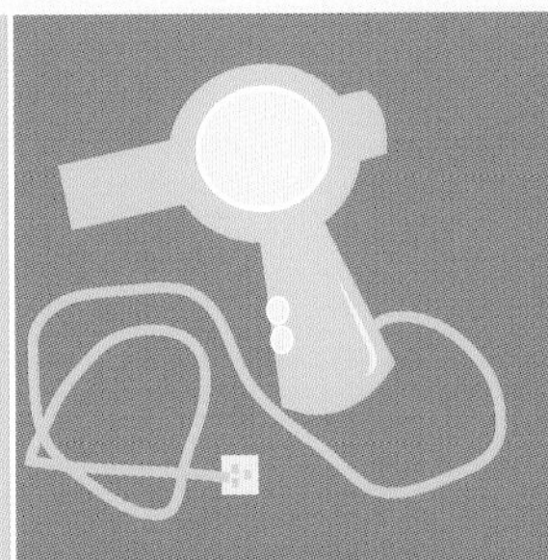

Not for a while.

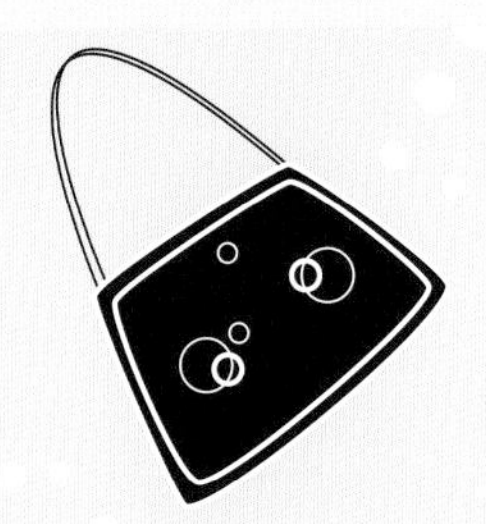

You may have problems getting there, but yes.

Love is in the air.

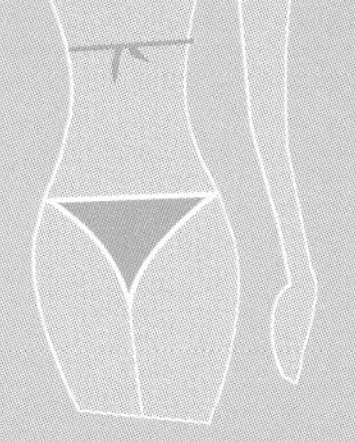

However much you want to, it's not a good idea.

It looks like you may have to borrow it.

Don't push it away. Deal with it.

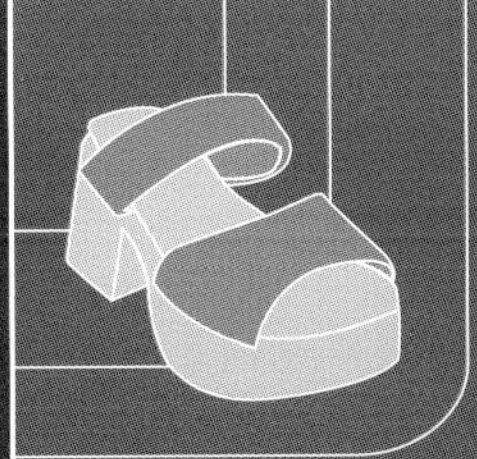

Yes, but not about anything important.

Do what you did the last time.

Not this time.
Something given to you by someone special.
You may not stay in any job long enough to really build your success.
Not for a while, but you're too much of a perfectionist!
Your friend has not forgotten; be patient.
They do. Remind them that you're there.
Not for a little while.
Yes, if you look with different eyes.
They can't stop thinking about you.

Most people really like you.

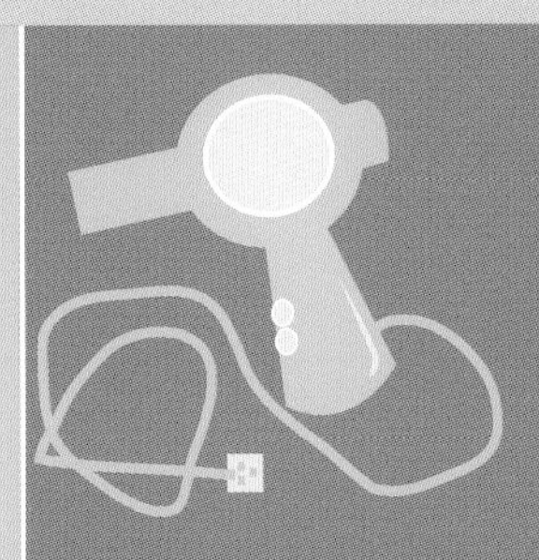

You may find that silence is harder to bear.

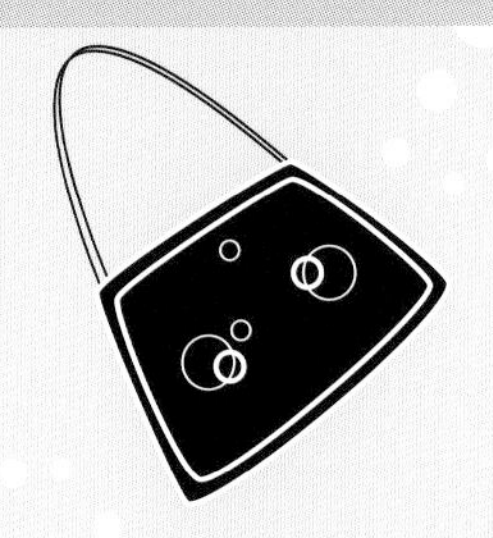

A big change.

It was a good one, but it may not turn out exactly as you expect.

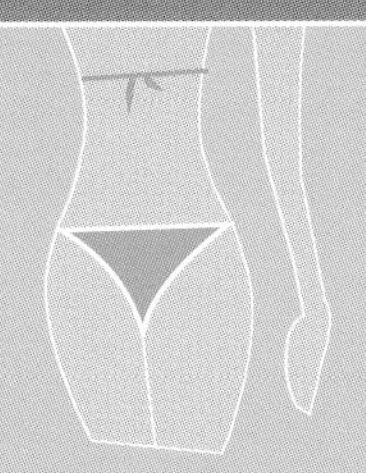

Try helping around the house.

Relax. You will sail through it.

Yes. Have a little more confidence.

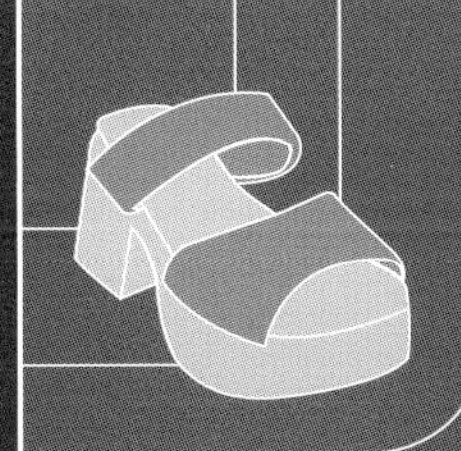

Calm down, and everyone will be nice again.

Someone you love more than anything else.

It is on its way.

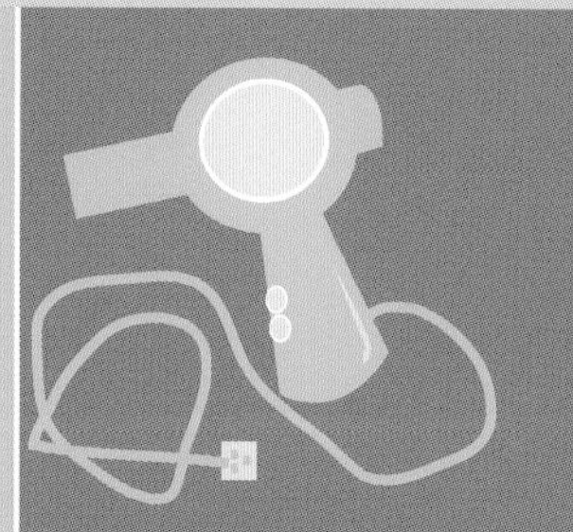

Very serious.

You will have a great time, and everything will be fine.

That is up to you.

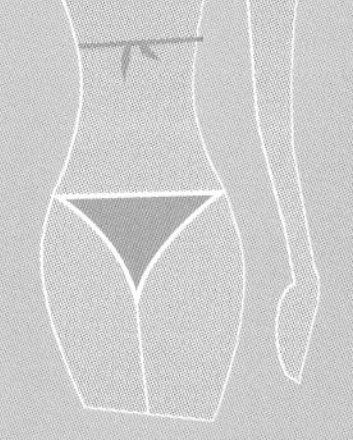

Not at all.

Go for a new style that works for you, and don't follow trends.

...... is your best friend, so go for it.

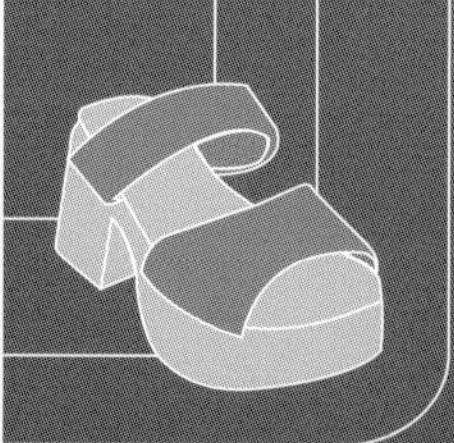

They like your image.

Because they don't know your good points yet.

Nothing lasts forever.

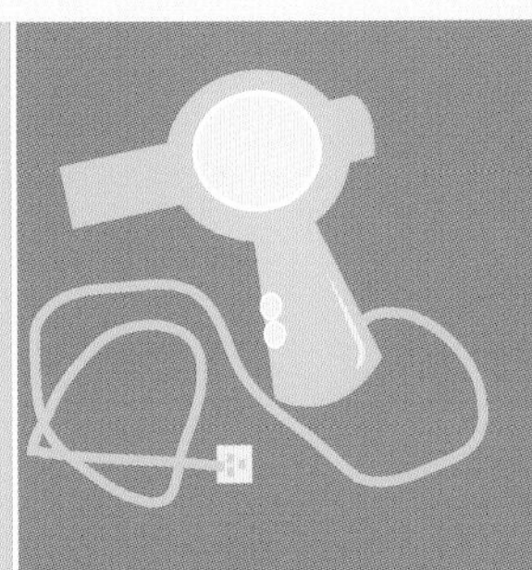

Hopefully, but not absolutely. Be flexible.

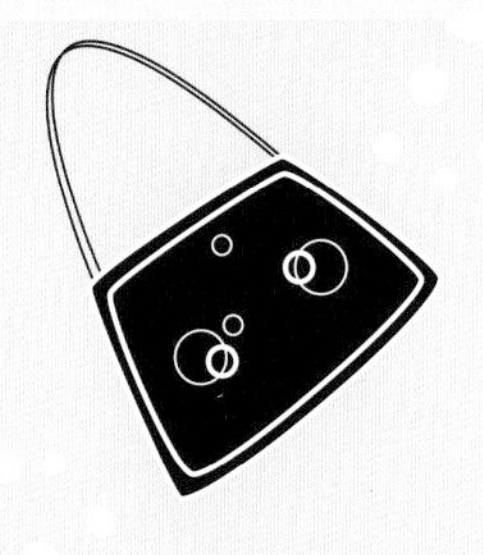

It could happen at any time now.

Yes, but it doesn't matter.

It will soon get much easier. Persevere.

Your friend needs cheering up, so you call.

A serious change at home.

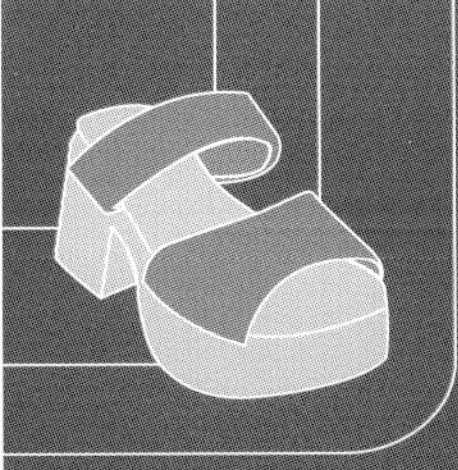

Give them space to make the next move.

It's a bad joke.

No. It will only end
up hurting you.

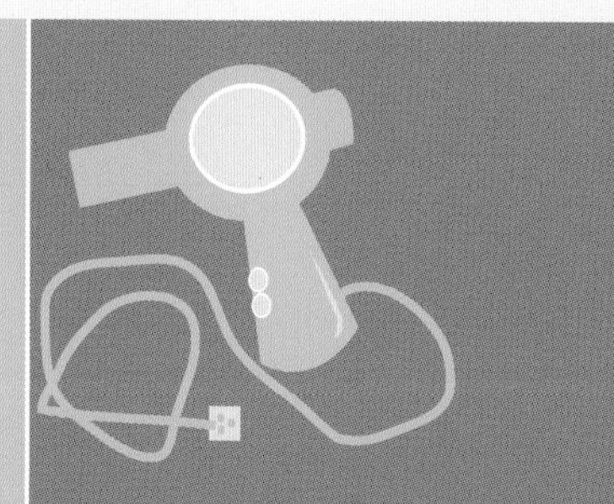

No. They care
about you too much.

Give them time to
come around to the idea.

Yes. Trust them.

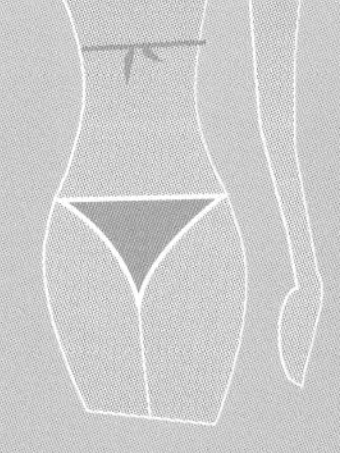

Yes. They are waiting
for the perfect moment.

Their mind is on other
things just now, but
they certainly like you.

Keep looking after your
skin and no one but you
will really notice them.

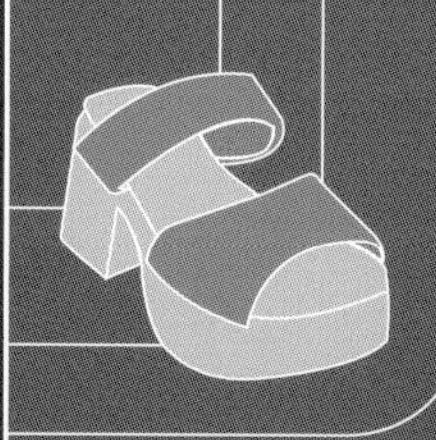

Long enough
to remember
for a long time.

Not enormously, but
you won't mind.

To you, absolutely.

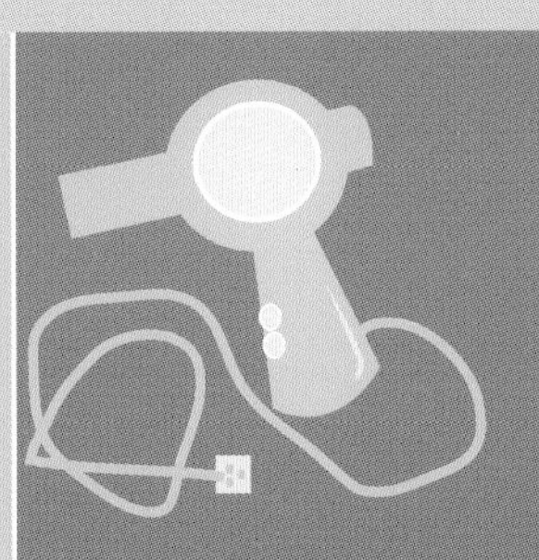

A few.

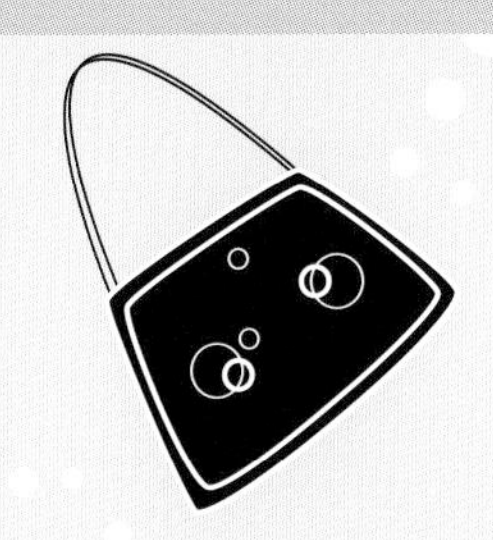

The trust is
already restored.

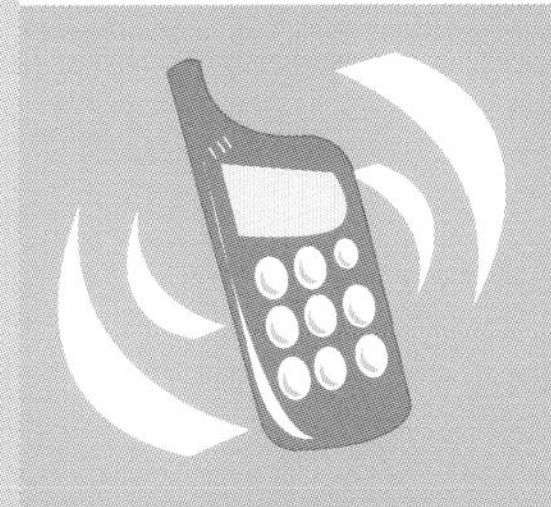

They may not
all be your own.

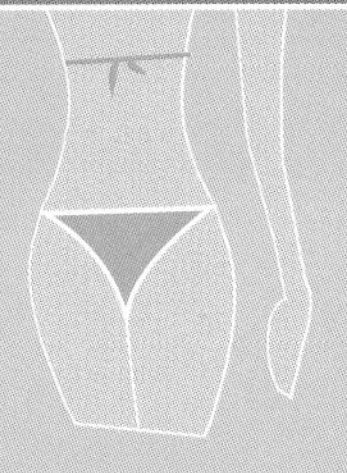

There will be a crush, but
nothing serious yet.

Go for it. All the
problems are behind you.

Yes. In the nick of time.

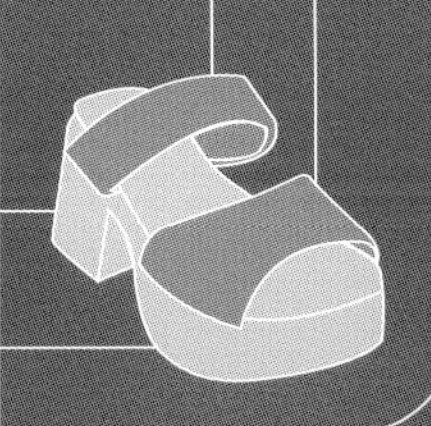

Believe in yourself
and it will start to
disappear.

No. Not about you.

Everything will be fine. You worry too much.

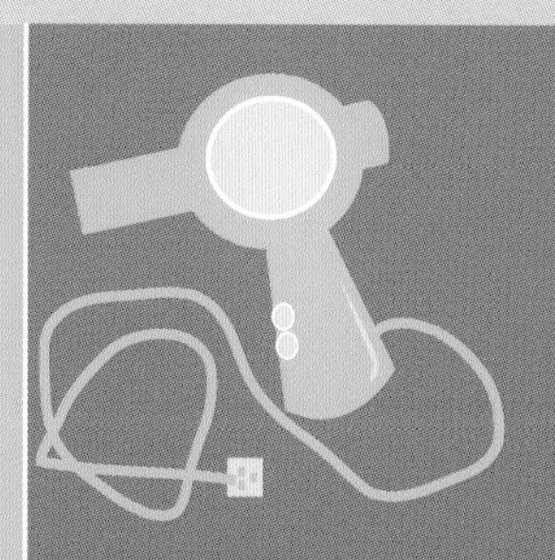

It is the best thing to do.

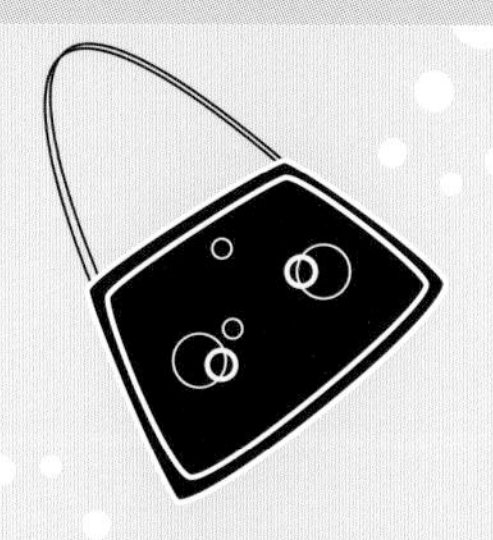

Some kind of star.

You must choose your career carefully first.

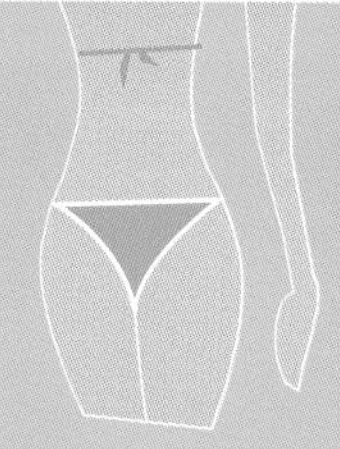

Yes, when you stop wishing you had someone else's.

No. I'm afraid it's gone.

That question has already been answered.

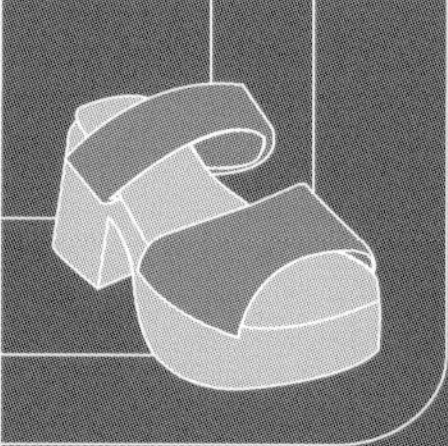

You know the answer.

Not this year.

Reasonably.
Some people think you're a little bossy.
They have said all they want to for now.
A new romance.
It was a wise one.
There is no way to make up for it, but they'll forgive in their own time.
It will be difficult at first, but you'll get into it and do well.
Yes, really well.
Ask your friends.

Always. It's part of your personality.
It may take a little more time.
Fairly serious.
Any problems will go unnoticed.
Something small will change.
Only a little bit, so you shouldn't worry about it.
Yes. Thin out your wardrobe and start over with a fresh look.
Not while things are so heated between you.
They are using you.

Only if you do something about it.

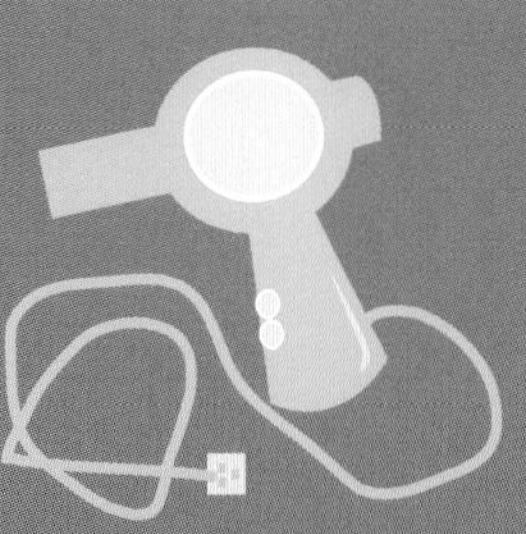

It will come to a crashing end soon, and something new will start.

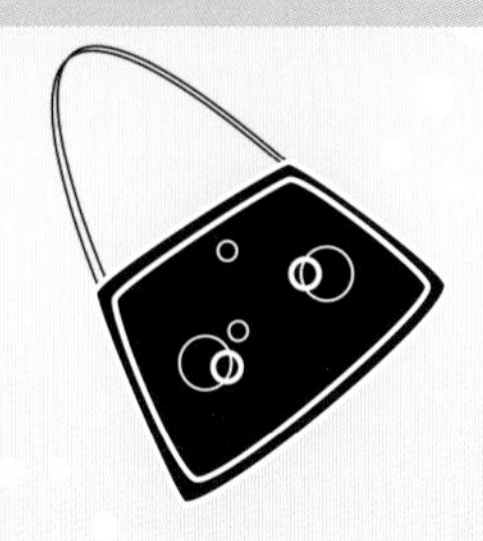

No, but hope for the best.

See your doctor and talk about it.

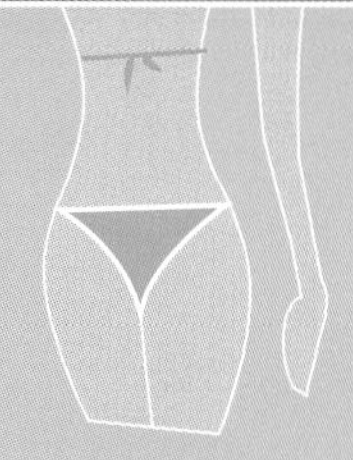

No. They really like you a lot.

No, not for a while; but, if you change your attitude toward it, this will help.

Your friend is shy.

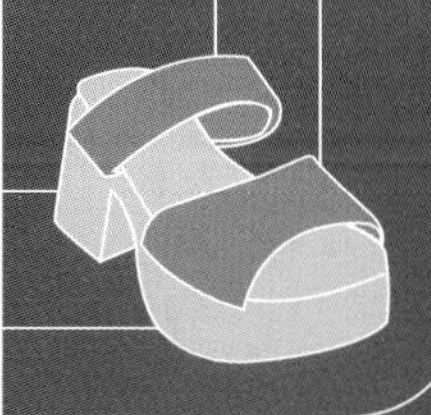

Two changes – one not so good, and the other, wonderful.

Show up at the same place, but act cool.

They're just worrying about you.

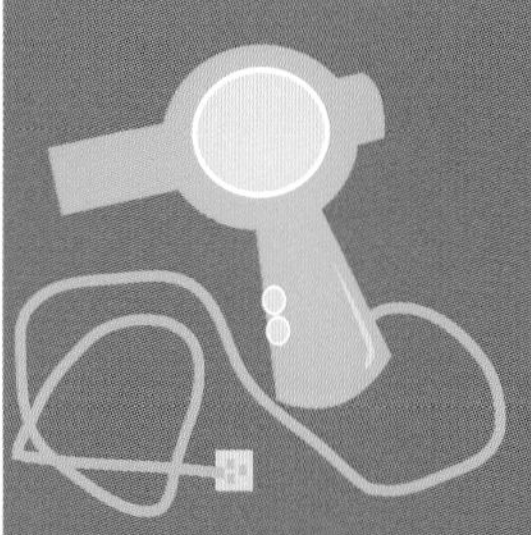

You know this person is not the most reliable witness.

Think about how your suspicions were aroused.

You know they already do, and are giving you more freedom.

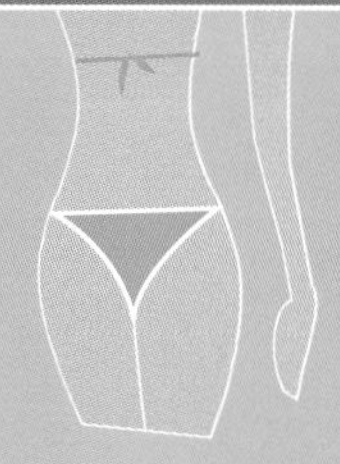

Not really. It may be up to you to solve.

It is your turn to call them.

Time has made you forget how much.

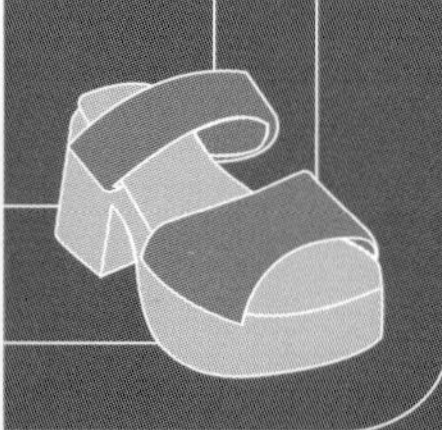

Yes. If they're bad at the moment, you may have a food allergy.

Soon you will enjoy a different happiness.

Soon.
No, but very sexy!
Of course not. They have too much good sense.
Never entirely.
Three.
Be prepared for a serious kiss.
Don't let your friends put you off; it'll be great fun.
Wait. Your target won't go anywhere. You have time.
Try to ignore it.

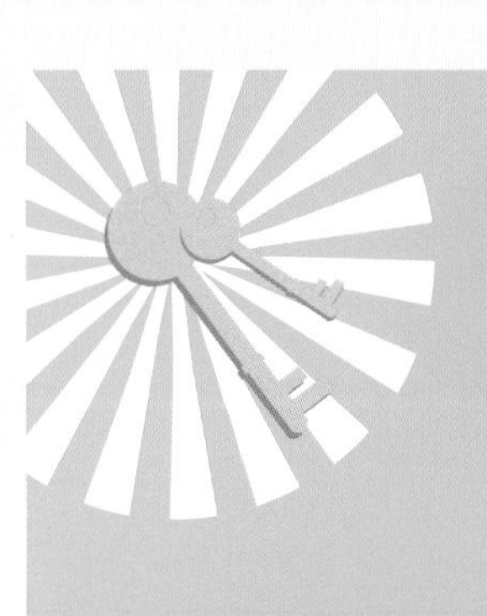

They will be.

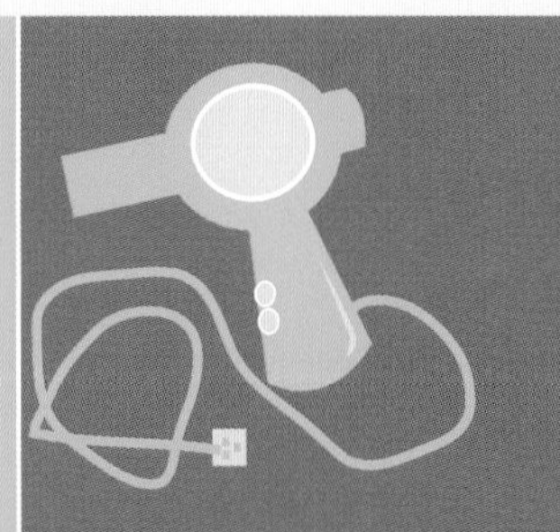

Not for a little while. Be strong.

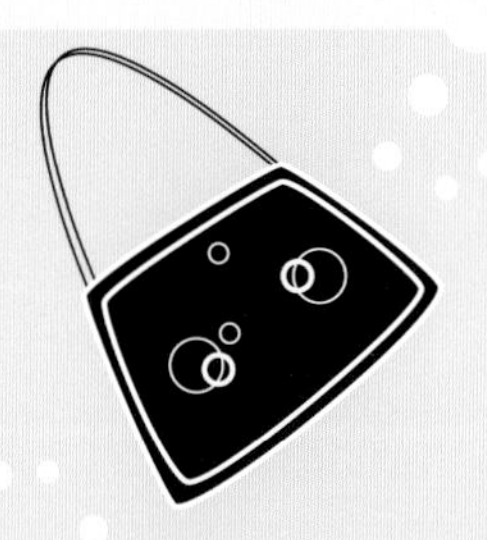

It was not your fault; but yes, if you can.

Something you can put on your key ring.

You will work hard at it and be very successful.

Yes you will. You'll work hard to keep the shape you like.

Why don't you remind your friend?

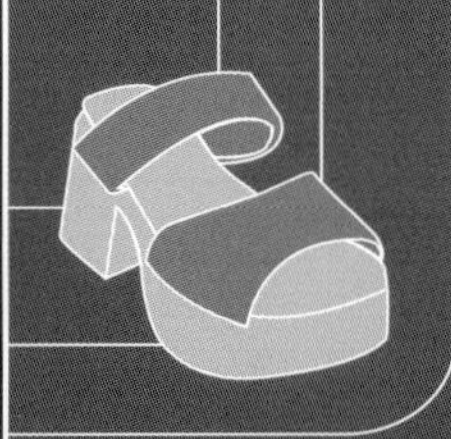

There should be no doubt that they do.

Not now. It would be too much trouble.

Maybe not.

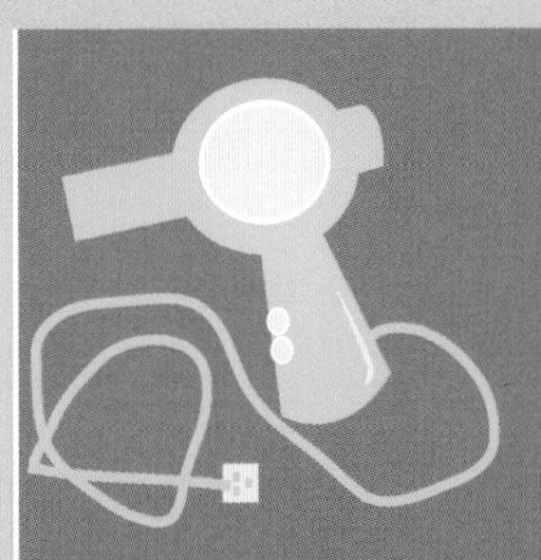

In your own right.

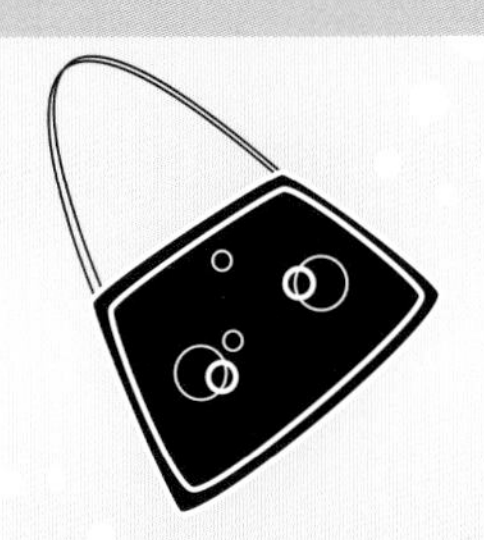

You're loved by all for your good temperament and sweetness.

If they stop tomorrow, they'll start again later.

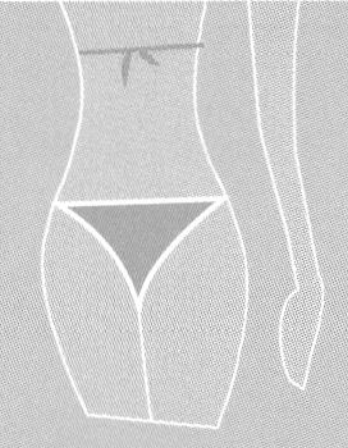

Not what you expect.

Your intentions were good, but the decision was not quite right!

By being sensitive to their feelings.

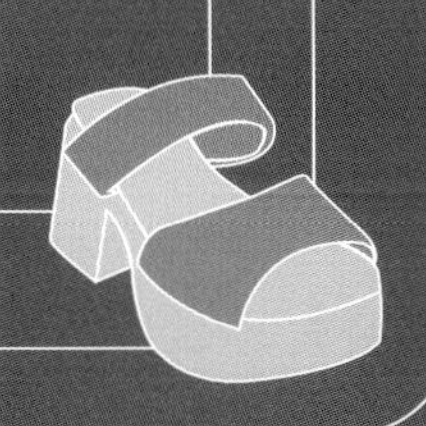

Afterward you may think it wasn't perfect, but it will work out well.

As well as can be expected.

Nothing too serious.

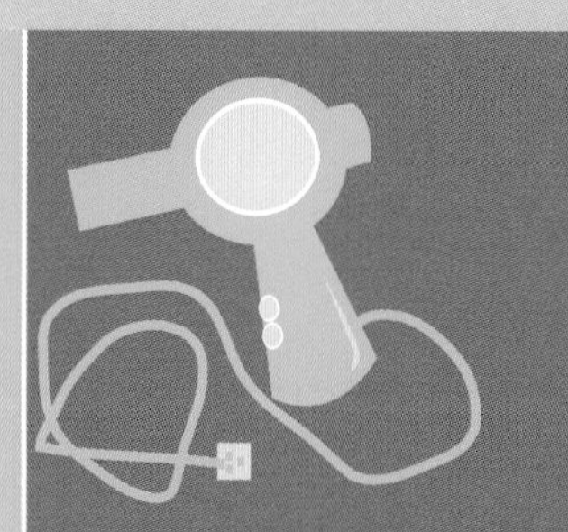

Not as much
as you want.

Be patient.

Don't waste any time
thinking about it.

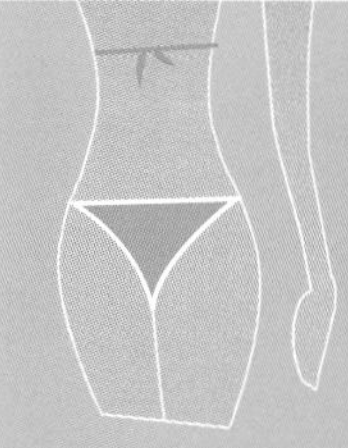

A few hitches will mean
things won't go smoothly,
but you'll still be happy.

There is a change coming
that you'll welcome,
but it will take a little while.

No. You have a
mature shape that
you will grow into.

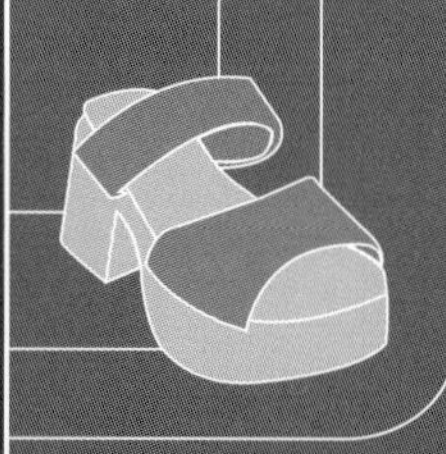

You look good in
everything you wear.

Yes.

Yes, in time. Let
things cool down.
Yes, but you should help
it along by being positive .
It may seem
like it, but it won't.
Definitely. It's a
good plan.
Not long from now.
You two have a
clash of tastes; that
won't change!
Yes. It already is
getting easier.
Your friend hasn't
had a chance.
Something lost,
something found.

By saying you're sorry.
You. You're not easy to understand just now!
Why not?
No, they wouldn't do that. Stop worrying.
Give them credit for how much freedom they do give you.
You know they can.
They have decided not to call.
Not any more. They have moved on, and so should you.
Of course they will, if you treat them with respect!

Confront them.

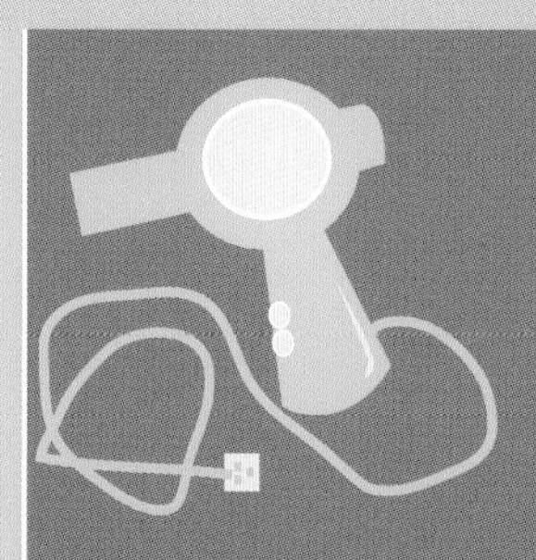

Yes, a lot of good luck!

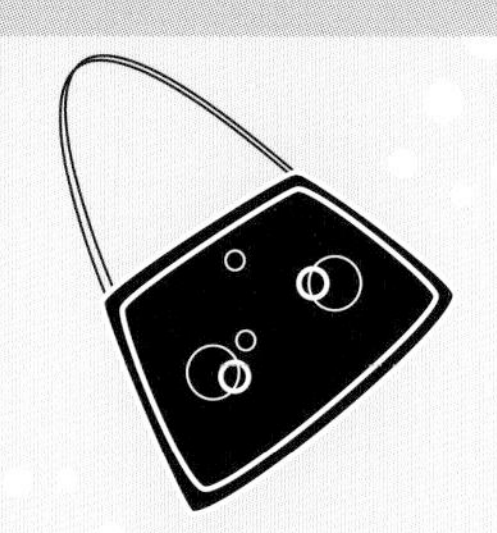

Very.

They know you better than that.

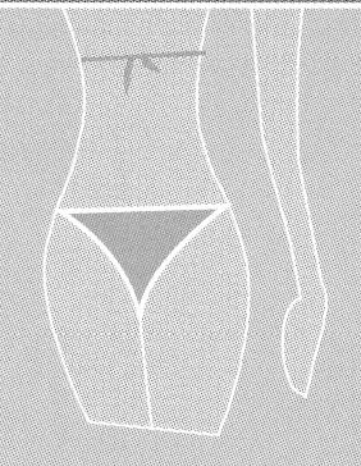

Yes, but there will always be some doubts in another friend's mind.

Yes, but all boys.

Your vacation may not be, but coming home will be exciting!

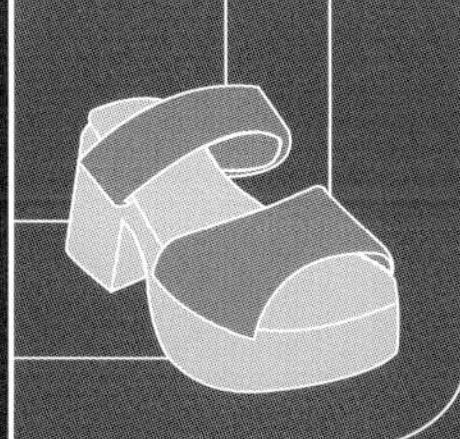

It could be embarrassing for you.

Sorry, not this time.

More than you notice them!

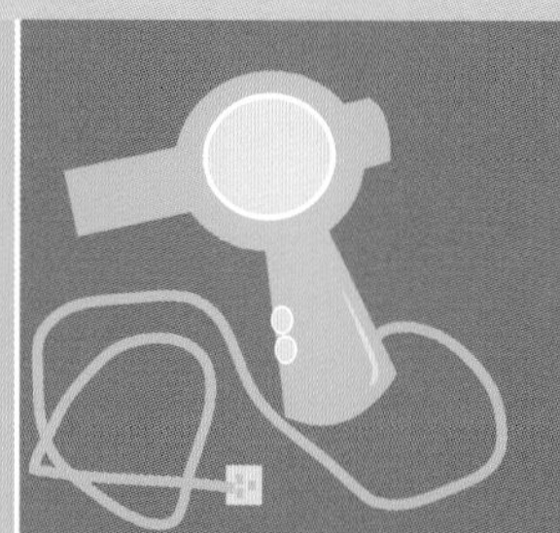

Only on the outside; actually, they're a little jealous.

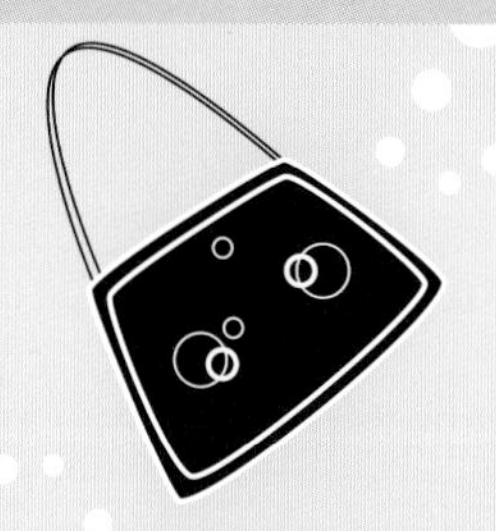

Yes, if you stay calm.

Don't blame yourself, but if you say sorry first, you're the bigger person.

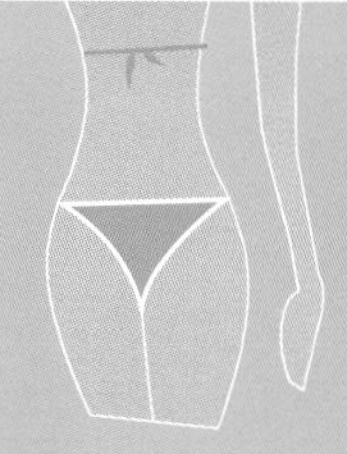

Something you are given at Easter that you cannot eat.

Decide that for yourself. If you want one, you must focus on it.

When you are older you will be a lot happier with it.

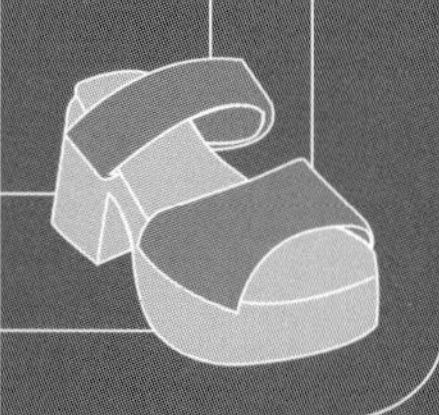

Your friend has already given it back.

Always and forever.

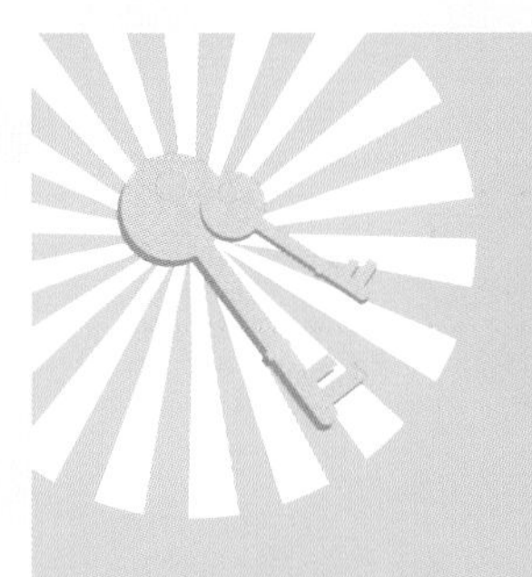

One too many admirers!

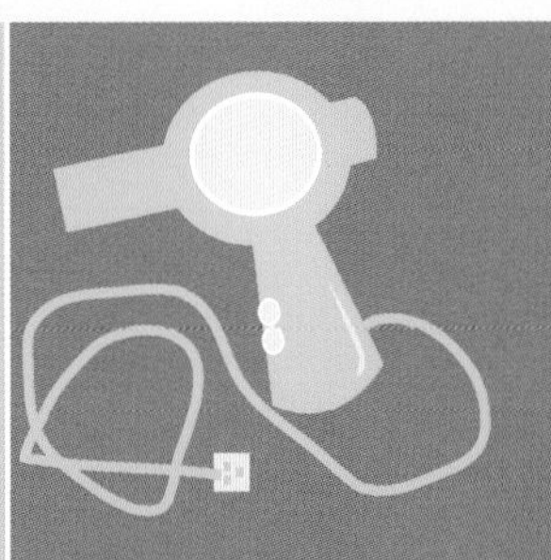

They already do, really.

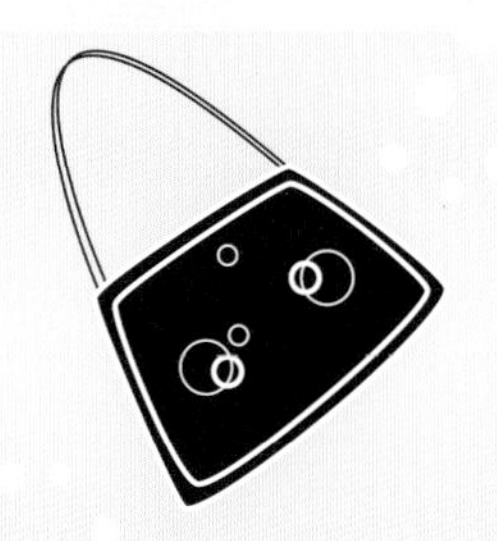

As famous as
you'll want to be.

The jealous ones think
you're snooty.

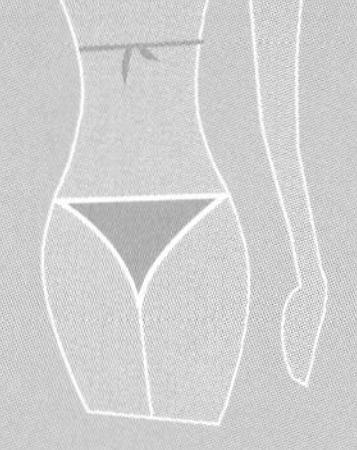

They will stop soon.
They are under a lot of
stress at the moment.

The experience
of a lifetime!

Yes, it will pay off
handsomely.

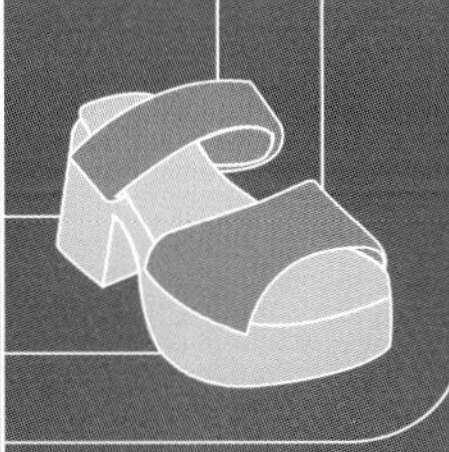

This may come up in
the future and they could
use it against you.

Something won't be quite
right but you may not be
sorry about that!

Jealousy.
Yes, just a few.
Do you even need to ask?
You'll have to wait a while longer.
Definitely, however strange that seems.
Don't worry. It will work out.
There is a change on the way, but it will take a few adjustments.
Lose a little weight by exercising and eating well, but it's not serious.
Stop copying others and find your own self-expression.

Not at all.

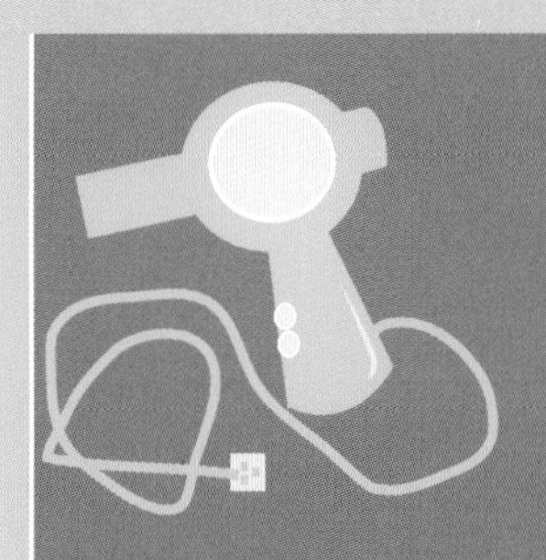

Not for a while,
but eventually.

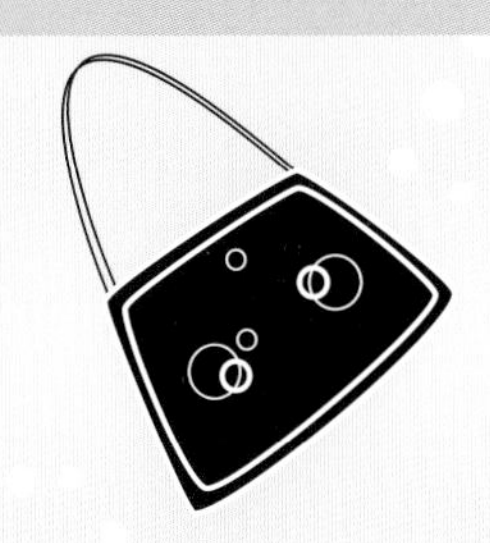

You have seen the worst.

It will last as
long as you let it.

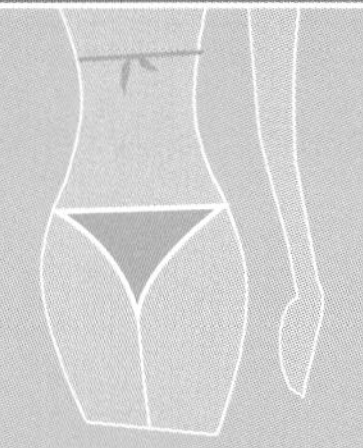

If you really want it
to, no one can stop you!

I think this is the wrong
question for you.

They like you a lot,
but don't know
how to show it.

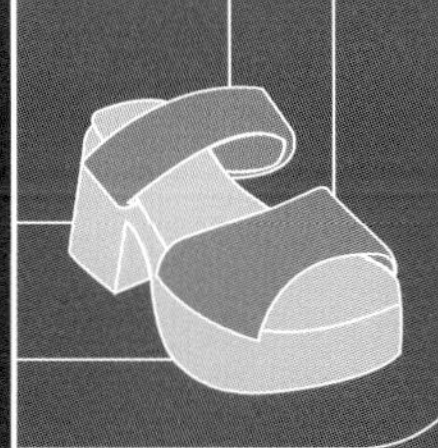

Adjust your attitude
toward it. You will find out
that it is fairly easy.

Your friend is being
watched too carefully.

Moderately.

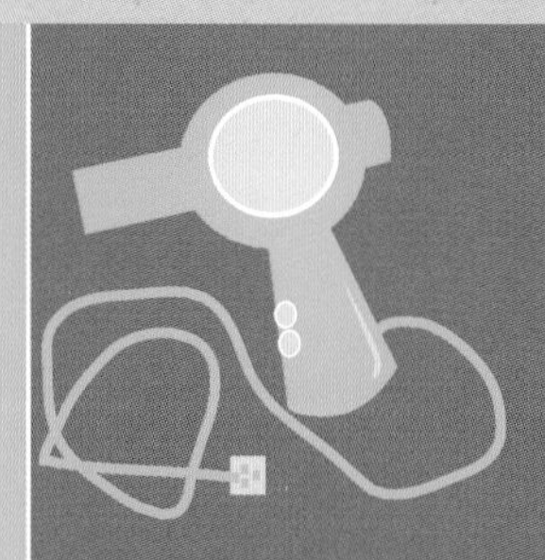

Use your brain and
a little humor.

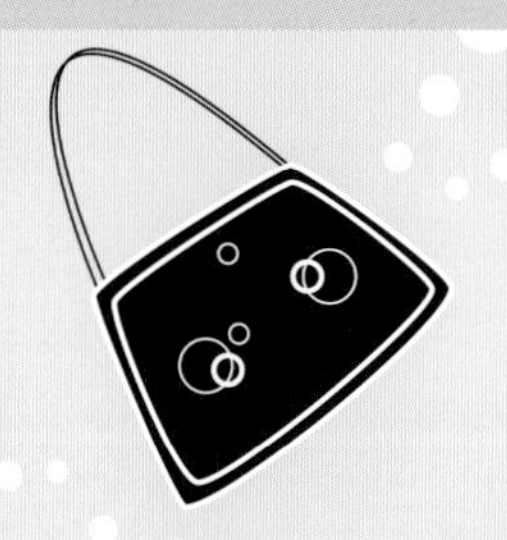

Your safety
and well-being.

You only ask this
because you don't want
to believe it!

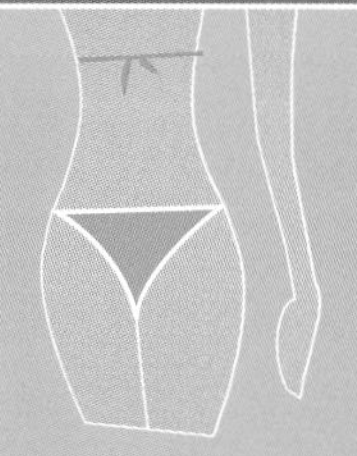

Yes, and you
know it too!

They will soon.

Maybe not, but be
sure to tell someone.

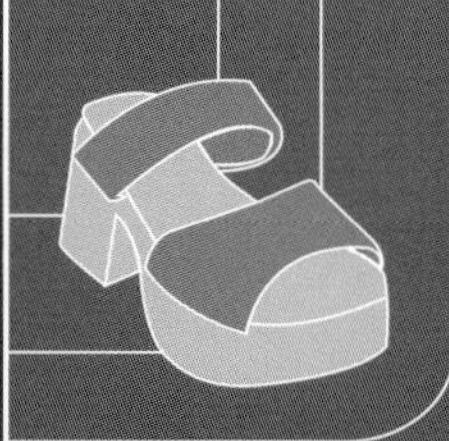

Yes, any minute.

Why do you doubt it?

No. You're too sensitive.

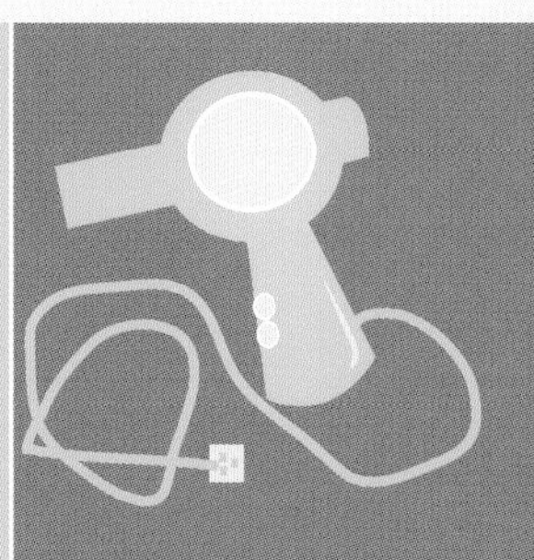

They will just stop very soon. Forget it.

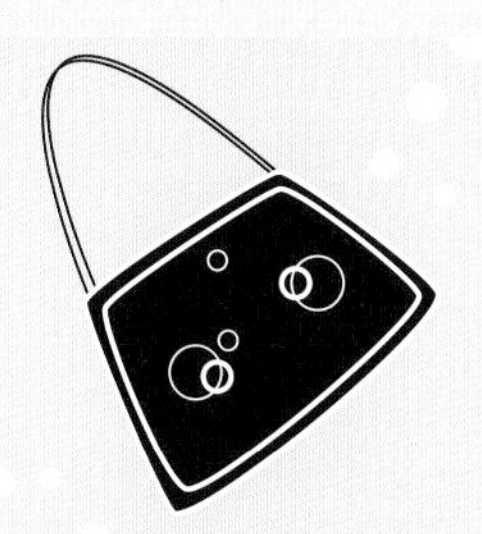

What do you mean by "luck"? Try to make your own luck.

It really doesn't matter: it will be love at first sight!

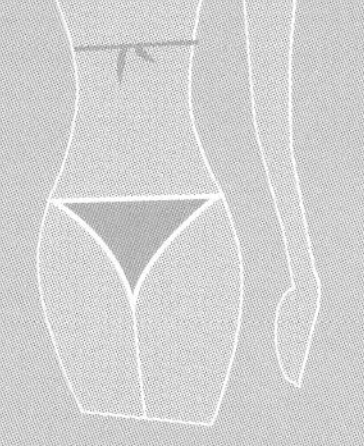

Only one.

On the outside perhaps, but never completely on the inside.

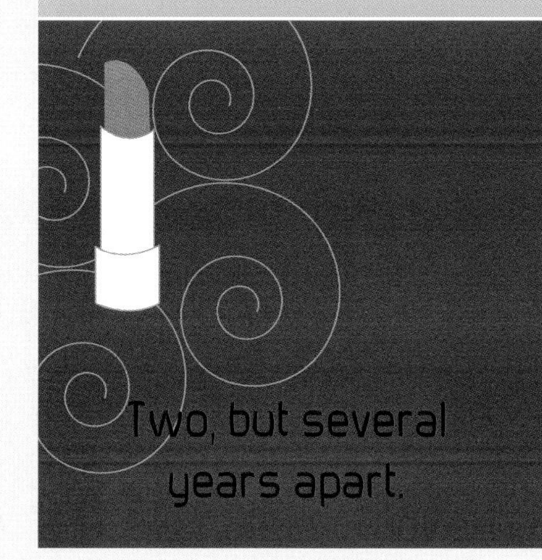

Two, but several years apart.

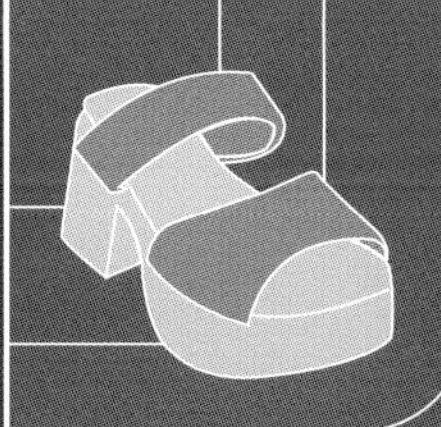

You'll be more than happy.

Go, and be the life of the party!

Published by Cedco Publishing in 2001
100 Pelican Way, San Rafael, CA 94901
www.cedco.com

First published in 2001 by Quadrille Publishing Limited
Alhambra House, 27-31 Charing Cross Road London WC2H 0LS

Publishing Director Anne Furniss
Creative Director Mary Evans
Design Coralie Bickford-Smith
Illustration Coralie Bickford-Smith
Editorial Assistant Katie Ginn
Production Nancy Roberts

Library of Congress Cataloging-in-Publication Data available

ISBN 0-7683-2500-5

Printed in Germany